THE **TESTING** SERIES

ADVANCED NUMERICAL REASONING
TESTS

DAVID ISAACS

THE **TESTING** SERIES
expert advice on interview preparation

Orders: Please contact How2become Ltd, Suite 2,
50 Churchill Square Business Centre, Kings Hill, Kent ME19 4YU.

Telephone: (44) 0845 643 1299 - Lines are open Monday to Friday 9am until 5pm.
You can also order via the email address info@how2become.co.uk.

ISBN: 9781907558290

First published 2011

Typeset for How2become Ltd by Molly Hill, Canada.

Printed in Great Britain for How2become Ltd by
Bell & Bain Ltd, 303 Burnfield Road, Thornliebank, Glasgow G46 7UQ.

CONTENTS

PREFACE

Thanks for your interest in the ultimate guide to passing numerical psycho-metric tests and congratulations on taking the next steps towards gaining that dream job.

The structure of this book takes you upon a journey which gradually improves your confidence in answering numerical psychometric test questions. It contains 51 realistic questions designed to imitate the real tests and 53 detailed answers with full explanations to match in order to improve your understanding of what is expected of you and how to answer the questions quickly and correctly every time.

I urge you not to sit the mock exam until you have gone through every example in the book as this will most likely damage your confidence before you have even started to build it up!. Remember that in order to improve, practice and persistence is the key.

Before we begin, I highly recommend investing in a scientific calculator if you have not done so already. Doing this will save you a lot of time during the exams and many of the time saving tips I have provided you throughout the book contain information on how to save time in the exam using a scientific calculator.

Where you see a number highlighted in grey, for example, **$4022.74** it is there because that particular number will shortly be used within an equation which follows. The idea is that if you see a number highlighted in grey within an equation, you will know where the number came from. I know exactly what it's like trying to find where a number which appears in an equation came from and I hope this simplifies the process for you.

I will be with you every step of the way during this book and I wish you every success in gaining the job of your dreams.

Let the journey to success begin right here and right now.

David Isaacs
Author

QUESTION 1
DATA
INTERPRETATION

QUESTION 1A

The image below shows the cumulative number of births in various locations across the UK over a period of 4 months.

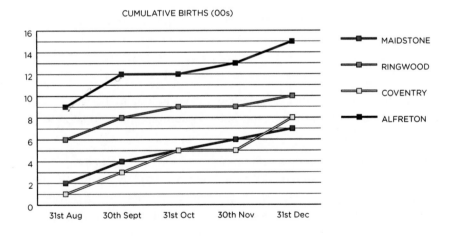

CUMULATIVE BIRTHS (00s)

For the month of September, how many births took place in Maidstone?

a. 9
b. 1,200
c. 3,000
d. 200
e. 250

SOLUTION TO QUESTION 1A

NOTE: *The graph data is cumulative. What this means is that the data is increasing by successive addition for every month, starting with the month of September.*

The following is a good explanation of how cumulative graphs, such as the one above function. Assume you get an income paid into your bank every week. On the first week you get paid, you spend nothing from your earnings and then get paid again the second week, but an unspecified amount. Your income for the second week could be higher or lower than your earnings on the first week. A cumulative data graph would not tell you directly how much income you have made for the second week, but what it would tell you directly is how much income you have had in total over the two weeks.

Referring back to the question, sadly, this means that it is not simply a matter of reading straight off the graph to see how many births took place in September, which I am sure every reader would no doubt prefer it to be!. The procedure to get the correct answer is outlined below:

For the month of September, in Maidstone, I need to look at the two points located above 31st August and 30th September and then find the difference between them:

Follow the 30th September upwards from the x-axis* until it hits the Maidstone curve, the data point sits on the number 4 in the y-axis*. Do the same for the 31st August. Following it upwards until it hits the Maidstone curve reveals that the data point lies on the number 2 in the y-axis. Both points are circled in the diagram below for clarity.

The x-axis is the horizontal component of any graph and the y-axis is the vertical component of any graph.

 THE **TESTING** SERIES

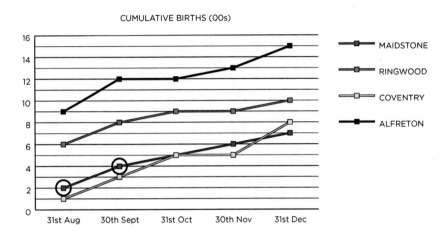

CUMULATIVE BIRTHS (00s)

To find the difference, subtract both points from each other: **4-2=2**

The next thing I need to consider is that the title of the graph tells me that all numbers used in the graph are shortened by two zeros [Cumulative Births (00s)]. So, for the difference I just calculated between the two points above 30th September and 31st August, the number 2 becomes 200.

This is the answer to part 1a: **d. 200**

QUESTION 1B

How many births, in total, took place in Ringwood during the months of September, October and November?

a. 300
b. 3
c. 250
d. 900
e. 750

SOLUTION TO QUESTION 1B)

For this question it is important you understand that the graph is cumulative, the definition of which is given in the solution to part "a".

Looking at the Ringwood curve on the graph, I need to find how many births took place each month, starting from September and ending in November, as the question requests.

To do this, I follow the same procedure shown in part a), but this time there are an extra 2 months to carry it out for:

BIRTH'S AT RINGWOOD IN SEPTEMBER:

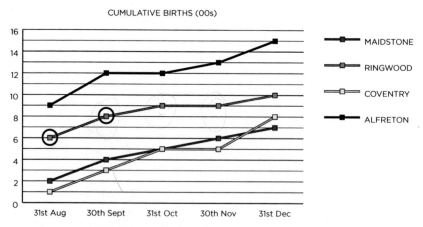

CUMULATIVE BIRTHS (00s)

To calculate the birth's at Ringwood in September, subtract the two points circled in the above graph: **8-6=2**

The title of the graph tells me that the numbers in the data are shortened by

two zeros so I now add two zeros to this, which brings the number of births at Ringwood in September to 200.

BIRTH'S AT RINGWOOD IN OCTOBER:

The same procedure as shown above is followed; the only difference is that the numbers being subtracted are taken from the October value on the graph for Ringwood, circled below:

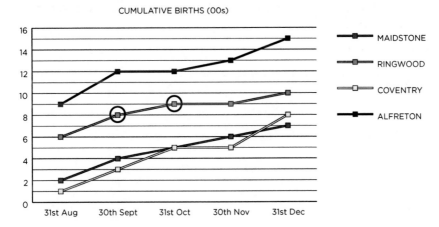

CUMULATIVE BIRTHS (00s)

Calculation for number of Births at Ringwood in October: **9-8=1**

Adding the two zeros to the end of this gives 100 births at Ringwood in October.

BIRTH'S AT RINGWOOD IN NOVEMBER:

Following the same procedures shown above, and subtracting the two circled points below leads to a figure of zero: **9-9=0**

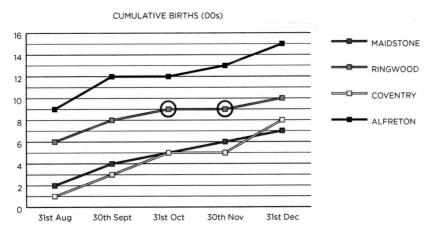

CUMULATIVE BIRTHS (00s)

This means that at Ringwood, in the month of November, there were no births.

BIRTHS AT RINGWOOD IN SEPTEMBER, OCTOBER AND NOVEMBER:

To calculate the total number of births, simply add each month's births, calculated above:

There were 200 births in September, 100 births in October and 0 births in November, the total is therefore:

200+100+0=300

The answer to question 1b is therefore: **a. 300**

QUESTION 1C

Assuming that the birth trend for Coventry seen in the month of December continues into January, how many births will take place in total during the months of November, December and January for Coventry?

a. 30

b. 600

c. 6

d. 300

e. 150

SOLUTION TO QUESTION 1C

This question is asking me to assume 'that the birth trend for Coventry seen in the month of December continues during the month of January.' If this were to be drawn on the cumulative graph it would look like the following graph:

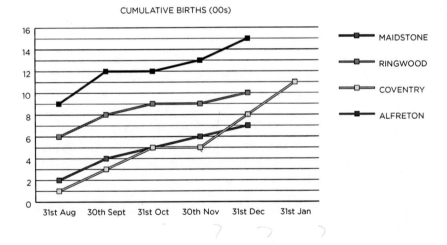

CUMULATIVE BIRTHS (00s)

It can now be seen from the above graph that if the birth trend for Coventry seen in December continues in the month of January, there would be 300 births in January, the same number of births seen in the month of December.

However, during the actual test, it would not be wise to draw out a graph due to time constraints. I will therefore now outline the procedure and thinking you should follow during the actual timed test below:

During the month of December for Coventry, there were 300 births. This was calculated by subtracting the two circled points shown in the graph below:

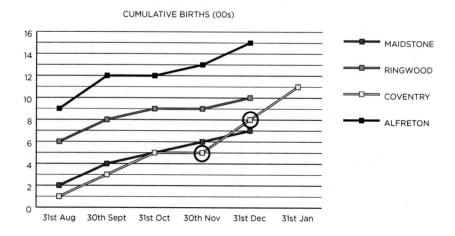

CUMULATIVE BIRTHS (00s)

8-5=3

The next step is to add two zero's to the end of the 3 as the title of the graph states that every number is shortened by two zeros, to give 300. Because the question states that it should be assumed the December birth trend for Coventry is continued in January, this can only mean that there were 300 births in January also, bringing the Coventry line to the 11 mark on the y-axis at the end of the month of January as shown in the graphs above.

The next step is to calculate the number of births for Coventry during the month of November.

Fortunately, there is a flat line representing the number of births in November for Coventry, which means that there were no births during this month.

Don't just take my word for it, see for yourself. The calculation would be to subtract the two points circled on the graph below:

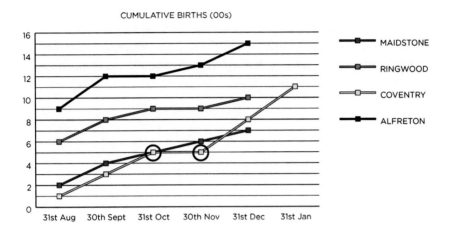

The calculation is: **5-5=0 births**

The next and final step to take is to add the number of births that took place in the months of November, December and January for Coventry:

0+300+300=600 births

Therefore, the answer to question 1c is: **b. 600 births** took place during the months of November, December and January for Coventry.

QUESTION 1D

If the trend in the number of births seen for Alfreton in the month of November continues into the month of December, what reduction in births will Alfreton have had for the month of December compared to what the data currently shows?

a. 300
b. 1,200
c. 100
d. 1,500
e. 290

SOLUTION TO QUESTION 1D

This question requires an assumption that the trend in the number of births seen for Alfreton in the month of November continues into the month of December. If this were to be the case, the difference between the original graph and the graph that includes this assumption would look like:

ORIGINAL GRAPH (Note the 31st December point for Alfreton)

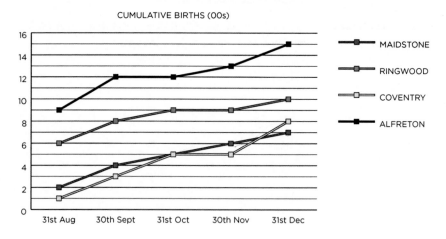

CUMULATIVE BIRTHS (00s)

GRAPH INCLUDING ASSUMPTION (Note the change on the 31st December point for Alfreton, it has reduced from hitting the y-axis at 15 to hitting it at 14)

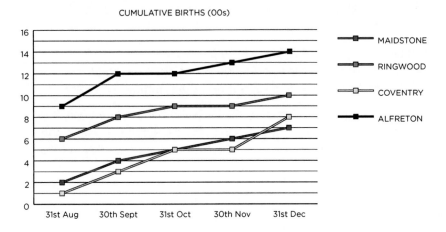

CUMULATIVE BIRTHS (00s)

The question is asking for the reduction in the number of births when comparing the two graphs. This can be solved in three easy steps:

1. I firstly need to know the original number of births in the month of December for Alfreton. This can be calculated using the original graph.

The procedure is to subtract the two points at the end and the beginning of the month. For the month of December in Alfreton, the calculation, using the original graph, is:

$$15-13=2$$

I also remember to add the two zero's to the end of this answer, giving 200 births originally in December for Alfreton.

2. The next step is to do the same again but this time for the graph which includes the assumption. So, for the month of December in Alfreton, the calculation, using the graph including the assumption, is:

$$14-13=1$$

Once again, I add the two zero's to the end of this answer because the title of the graph tells me that all numbers are shortened by two zero's [Cumulative Births (00's)], giving **100** births when there is an assumption that the trend of November is followed in December for Alfreton.

3. The final step required is to calculate the reduction in the number of births for Alfreton in December when assuming that the trend seen in November is continued into December for Alfreton. This can be achieved through the following calculation:

Original number of births *[found from the original graph]* -
Number of births with the assumption *[found from the graph including assumption]* = **The reduction in the number of births**

I calculated the original number of births in December for Alfreton in step 1 and I calculated the number of births with the assumption in December for Alfreton in step 2. I therefore have everything required to carry out the calculation:

200-100=100

The answer to 1d is a reduction of **c. 100 births.**

IMPORTANT POINTS

- Always check the title of any graph as it may reveal clues. In this case the clues were 'Cumulative' and '(00's)'.

- When there is a key on the graph, always make sure that you are following the curve that the question has asked you to use e.g. Part a) requires the use of the 'Maidstone' curve and using any other curve will not give you the answer required.

Remember that this is a timed test. There will not be time to draw your own diagram as I have done in the answers. The reason I did was so that you can grasp the concept of what's actually happening. In the real exam, you are expected to do the calculations very quickly and you will need to picture things in your mind, without drawing anything. With practice, which this book provides you plenty of, it will happen naturally.

QUESTION 2
PIE CHARTS & PERCENTAGE QUESTIONS

QUESTION 2A

The following chart gives the approximate population data for China, India and U.S.A.

POPULATION PIE CHART

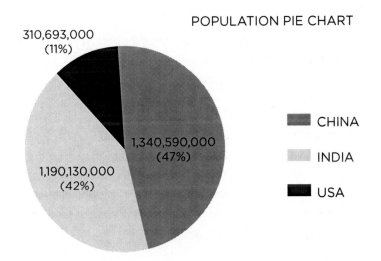

310,693,000
(11%)

1,340,590,000
(47%)

1,190,130,000
(42%)

CHINA

INDIA

USA

China's population makes up approximately 17.5% of the world population. What is the approximate population of the world?

a. 7,660,514,286

b. 6,697,254,041

c. 7,643,229,632

d. 8,528,132,994

e. Cannot Say

SOLUTION TO QUESTION 2A

In order to calculate the approximate population of the world, I need to know what information I currently have to work with. So the first thing I check is what information is displayed in the pie chart and the question itself.

I have the population of China, which is **1,340,590,000** from the pie chart and I also have the fact that China's population makes up **17.5%** of the world population, which was given in the question.

From these two pieces of vital information, I can now calculate the approximate population of the world. Before I do so, I would like to explain my approach and way of thinking towards such questions so that you can see exactly how I go about tackling such questions:

Firstly, as a nice easy example, I will need you to imagine an orange grove full of trees. (This will all make sense shortly, I assure you!). Within this orange grove, there are 100 oranges grown in total from all the trees. A particular tree, let's call it tree A, produces 10 out of the 100 oranges grown within the perimeter of the orange grove.

The percentage that tree A contributes towards the total amount of oranges in the grove is simply 10 out of 100, which in mathematical terms looks like:

$$\frac{10}{100} = 0.1$$

To convert the 0.1 into a percentage I multiply it by 100:

$$0.1 \times 100 = 10\%$$

MATHEMATICAL TIP: *Any decimal can be converted into a percentage by multiplying it with 100 and adding a '%' sign at the end. To convert a percentage back into a decimal, divide it with 100.*

This now tells me, from a percentage perspective that tree A produces 10% of the total oranges within the orange grove.

Now that you know this, it is easy to solve the following example, designed to be similar to question 2a.:

ORANGE TREE EXAMPLE

Orange tree A produces 10 oranges, which is 10% of the total oranges for the orange grove. What is the total amount of oranges produced in the orange grove?

SOLUTION TO THE ORANGE TREE EXAMPLE

I am not told that the orange grove contains 100 oranges in total and therefore cannot use this or assume it in any of my working out. I will label the total oranges produced in the orange grove as '*x*' for now. Also, I cannot use 10% to multiply or divide anything with directly, so the first thing I need to do is convert the 10% into a decimal:

$$10\% = \frac{10}{100} = 0.1$$

Next, I know from above that the mathematical relationship between the percentage of oranges tree A produces and the total amount produced in the orange grove, '*x*', is:

$$\frac{\text{Oranges produced by tree A only}}{\text{Total oranges produced in the entire orange grove}} = \frac{10}{x} = 0.1$$

The equation can now be solved for '*x*' by rearranging:

$$x = \frac{10}{0.1} = 100$$

This is the solution to the orange tree example; the total amount of oranges produced in the orange grove is **100**.

Now, returning to the question, comparing this situation to question 2a., imagine that the world population is the total amount of oranges produced in the orange grove *x*, and China is the orange tree A, containing 10 oranges.

Hopefully question 2a. will not appear as scary now that you have gone through an example using two digit numbers rather than 10 digit numbers! The good news is that the method of solving such questions does not vary when using longer numbers, so I can now proceed to apply this exact method for the larger numbers in question 2a.

So, following the same procedure as for the Orange Tree example, I firstly need to change the percentage given in the question, into a decimal:

$$17.5\% = \frac{17.5}{100} = 0.175$$

Next, using the same thinking as the orange tree example, let x represent the world population and the following calculation leads to the solution of question 2a.:

$$\frac{\text{Population of China}}{\text{World Population}} = \frac{1,340,590,000}{x} = 0.175$$

Note that when the population of china is divided by world population, it gives the proportion that China contributes towards the total world population, which is 17.5%. This is the same as knowing what proportion of oranges tree A produces for the entire orange grove which was 10%.

The world population 'x' can now be found by rearranging the equation to give a final calculation of:

$$x = \frac{1,340,590,000}{0.175} = 7,660,514,286$$

The answer to question 2a is **a. 7,660,514,286**

QUESTION 2B

The following chart gives the approximate population data for China, India and U.S.A.

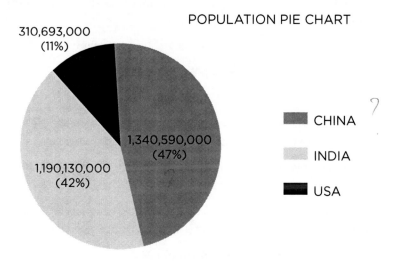

POPULATION PIE CHART

310,693,000 (11%)

1,340,590,000 (47%)

1,190,130,000 (42%)

CHINA

INDIA

USA

India's unemployed population is approximately twice that of the unemployed population of China and 113,052,032 more than the U.S.A's unemployed population of 14,291,878. What is the approximate unemployed population of China?

a. 65,333,214
b. 57,645,370
c. 57,642,170
d. 63,671,965
e. 58,455,232

SOLUTION TO QUESTION 2B.

The key point to note here is the fact that the question refers to unemployed populations rather than the total population of each country as is displayed in the pie chart.

This question states that India's unemployed population is half that of the unemployed population of China, without stating what the unemployed population of China actually is. This means that I am unable to use this information until I find out what either India's unemployed population is or China's.

However, the next piece of information provided in the question is that India's unemployed population is 14,530,807 more than the U.S.A's unemployed population of 14,291,878. This information now allows me to determine the unemployed population of India through the following calculation:

Unemployed population of India = USA's unemployed population + 113,052,032

= 14,291,898 + 113,052,032

= 127,343,930

Now that I know the unemployed population of India, I can use the information given to me in the first part of the question, which is:

India's unemployed population is approximately *twice* that of the unemployed population of China

All that is left to do in order to calculate the approximate unemployed population of China is to divide the unemployed population of India by 2:

Unemployed population of China=127,343,910÷2

=63,671,965

This is the final answer to question 2b, **d. 63,671,965**

QUESTION 2C

The following chart gives the approximate population data for China, India and U.S.A.

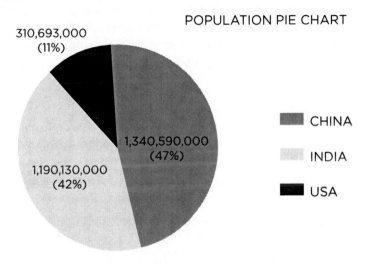

POPULATION PIE CHART

310,693,000 (11%)

1,340,590,000 (47%)

1,190,130,000 (42%)

CHINA

INDIA

USA

If China's population was once the same as India's, what is the percentage rise in China's population from then to now?

a. 42%
b. 47%
c. 12.6%
d. 15.8%
e. 14.3%

SOLUTION TO QUESTION 2C

IMPORTANT: *The percentages you see on the pie chart are there to show what proportion of the pie chart the population of each country is occupying and should not be used to determine the answer to part c. All it is there for is to show that each country has been given a fair slice of the pie, considering their populations. This is why China has the biggest percentage of 47% displayed on the pie chart, followed by India, 42% and lastly USA, with 11%, because it has the smallest population compared to the other two countries.*

A percentage difference, as the name suggests, is a difference between two numbers shown as a percentage.

The question requires me to perform a percentage difference calculation between the populations of India and China, assuming that the population of India shown on the pie chart is the 'old' population of China, which has now grown to become the current population of China shown on the pie chart. The following two methods can be used, pick the one you find easiest to remember and work with:

METHOD 1:

This method uses the **formula for percentage rise (increase)** given below:

$$\text{Percentage Increase} = \frac{\text{largest value - lowest value}}{\text{lowest value}} \times 100\%$$

- The 'largest' value for this question is the population of China shown on the pie chart, which is 1,340,590,000

- The 'lowest' value is the population of India shown on the pie chart, which is 1,190,130,000. This is because the question states that this was once the population of China, in other words, the population of India shown on the pie chart is the 'old' population of China.

FIRSTLY, subtract the 'largest' value from the 'lowest':

1,340,590,000−1,190,130,000=150,460,000

DIVIDE the answer to the subtraction above by the 'lowest' population, which in this case is the population of India:

150,460,000 ÷ 1,190,130,000=0.1264231...

CONVERT this decimal into a percentage by multiplying by 100 and adding a "%" sign at the end:

0.1264231...×100=12.6 4231...%

NOTE: The dots (...) that appear after the 1 for the decimal 0.1264321(...) and the percentage 12.64231(...) are there to show that they both continue, as you will see on your calculator display. Considering the percentage (12.6 4231...) will be rounded off at the dashed line, there is no use in writing out all the numbers as shown on the calculator display.

This percentage can be rounded off at the dashed line to give a 12.6% rise, which is the answer to question 2c.

METHOD 2:

DIVIDE the largest population by the lowest, in this case it is China's current population shown on the pie chart as 1,340,590,000, divided by China's 'old' population, in other words, India's current population shown on the pie chart as 1,190,130,000:

$$1,340,590,000 \div 1,190,130,000 = 1.1264231...$$

CONVERT the answer to the above division into a percentage by multiplying by 100 and adding a "%" sign at the end of it:

$$1.1264231... \times 100 = 112.64231\%$$

Finally, SUBTRACT 100% from this:

$$112.64231\% - 100\% = 12.6 \vdots 4231...\%$$

Once again, this percentage can be rounded off at the dashed line shown above, to give a **c. 12.6% rise,** which is the answer to question 2c.

NOTE: As the result from both method 1 and 2 is positive, this means that this is a percentage rise, however if the result turned out to be negative, this would mean a percentage decrease, in which case, the normal procedure to adopt is to ignore the negative sign and call it a percentage decrease.

QUESTION 3
DATA ANALYSIS AND PERCENTAGE GROWTH RATES

QUESTION 3A

2010 Population Data for Countries X, Y and Z

	POPULATION AT THE BEGINNING OF THE YEAR (millions)	UNEMPLOYMENT RATE (%)	ANNUAL POPULATION GROWTH RATE (%)
COUNTRY X	8	9.5	0.5
COUNTRY Y	9	8.2	0.2
COUNTRY Z	10	7.6	0.8

If the annual population growth rate for Country X remains constant, how many years are required for the population of COUNTRY X to increase by 120,601?

a. 3 years
b. 10 years
c. 2 years
d. 8 years

SOLUTION TO QUESTION 3A

I must firstly establish what needs to be worked out and what information is provided in order to solve the question. In this case the number of years taken to increase the population of COUNTRY X by 120,601 needs to be found. Below is an outline of what information the question provides:

• **The annual population growth for COUNTRY X remains constant**

This is telling me that the annual population growth for COUNTRY X in 2010 (which is 0.5% from the table) will remain 0.5%. This is not only for 2010 but for the foreseeable future. This means that in all calculations involving COUNTRY X, I must use 0.5% as its annual population growth rate.

• **How many years are required for the population of COUNTRY X to increase by 120,601?**

This part of question gives me two pieces of equally important information:

1. It has taken years rather than days, weeks or months for the population to increase. This important bit of information tells me that because it took years for the population to increase, I can use the annual (yearly) population growth for COUNTRY X in the calculations required for solving this question (method shown below).

2. The increase in the population of COUNTRY X is 120,601. This allows me to calculate what the population of COUNTRY X was and what the population of COUNTRY X has become after the increase of 120,601 and it is from these figures that I can calculate the solution to the question (method shown below)

The population at the beginning of the year 2010 for COUNTRY X is given in the table as 8 million (8,000,000)

To find the population for COUNTRY X the following year, i.e. at the beginning of the year 2011, the procedure is outlined below:

MATHEMATICAL TIP: *Whenever you come across a percentage and need to use it to find an increase, always convert that percentage into a decimal and add 1 to it.*

So, in this case, the annual population growth rate is 0.5%, converting this into a decimal using a calculator gives:

$$0.5\% \div 100 = 0.005$$

On some calculators, the answer to this calculation may appear on the display as 5×10–3 ; this is exactly the same as 0.005. The '×10–3' part is there to remind you that the decimal point goes back three places as shown below:

$$5 \times 10^{-3} = 0.005$$

The decimal moves 3 places backwards

Continuing, now that I have the decimal format of the percentage, I must add 1 to it in order to calculate an increase, as explained in the mathematical tip above:

$$1 + 0.005 = 1.005$$

Multiplying this with the population of COUNTRY X at the beginning of 2010 will give me the population at the beginning of 2011 for COUNTRY X:

$$1.005 \times 8{,}000{,}000 = 8{,}040{,}000$$

A TIME SAVING TIP *(only works using a scientific calculator): To save time in the exam, when inputting a number such as 8 million into a calculator, rather than typing in an 8 followed by six zeros, there is a button that can be pressed after inputting the number 8, called "EXP" on the calculator. Once the 8 is typed into the calculator and the "EXP" button pressed, the next number you press on the calculator will be how many zeros follow the number 8. So, for example, 8 million contains six zeros after the number 8, so I need to press 8, followed by "EXP", followed by the number 6, followed by the "=" [equal] button, which will display the same thing as typing in 8,000,000 but much faster and also you eliminate the risk of inputting too little or too many zeros by doing it this way which will save you points and time.*

To find the population increase for COUNTRY X between 2010 and 2011, simply calculate the difference between the two:

In 2011, the population of COUNTRY X is 8,040,000 and in 2010 it is 8,000,000:

$$8,040,000 - 8,000,000 = 40,000$$

This is not the answer I am looking for [I am looking for a 120,601 increase in population] and therefore it took more than a year for the population of COUNTRY X to increase by 120,601

Moving to the second year, 2012, the same annual increase is used, except this time the population at the beginning of 2011 for COUNTRY X is used rather than the population at the beginning of 2010 as was previously used:

$$\text{Population of COUNTRY X at the beginning of 2012} = 1.005 \times 8,040,000$$

$$= 8,080,200$$

Once again calculating the population increase for COUNTRY X between 2011, a population of [8,040,000] and 2012, a population of [8,080,200]:

$$8,080,200 - 8,040,000 = 40,200$$

In total, over the 2 years from 2010 to 2012 there has been a population increase of:

$$40,000 + 40,200 = 80,200$$

Again, this is not the answer I am looking for and therefore it took more than two years for the population of COUNTRY X to increase by 120,601

Now moving on to the third year, 2013, the same calculation takes place with the exception that the population to be used in this calculation is the population at the beginning of 2012 for COUNTRY X, which was calculated above to be 8,080,200:

$$\text{Population of COUNTRY X at the beginning of 2013} = 1.005 \times 8,080,200$$

$$= 8,120,601$$

Now I must once again calculate the population increase for COUNTRY X between 2012, a population of [8,080,200] and 2013, a population of [8,120,601]:

$$8,120,601 - 8,080,200 = 40,401$$

 THE **TESTING** SERIES

In total, over the 3 years from 2010 to 2013 there has been a population increase of:

$$40{,}000 + 40{,}200 + 40{,}401 = 120{,}601$$

Finally, this is the answer I have been waiting for. Therefore, the answer to question 3a is 3 years.

QUICKEST METHOD:

The above method would consume precious time during the real exam and was provided for explanation purposes and as a second option to those who may prefer solving the question using that particular method. The quickest way to solve part a) is given in the steps below:

1. Add 120,601 to 8 million, which gives:

$$120{,}601 + 8{,}000{,}000 = 8{,}120{,}601$$

2. Starting with 8,000,000 and increasing the population by the annual population growth rate year on year, it is possible to count how many years it will take for the population of COUNTRY X to reach 8,120,601 as demonstrated below:

AIM: To find how many years it took for the population of COUNTRY X to reach 8,120,601 starting from the 2010 population for COUNTRY X of 8,000,000. (Remember that the 1.005 represents the annual population growth rate)

Population for COUNTRY X (2010): 8,000,000

Population after 1 year (2011): $1.005 \times 8{,}000{,}000 = 8{,}040{,}000$

✗ (The population is not 8,120,601 after 1 year so I continue until it is 8,120,601)

Population after 2 years (2012): $1.005 \times 8{,}040{,}000 = 8{,}080{,}200$

✗ (Getting closer but not quite 8,120,601 yet)

Population after 3 years (2013): $1.005 \times 8{,}080{,}200 = 8{,}120{,}601$

✓ **Therefore it will take 3 years for the population of COUNTRY X to become 8,120,601 which is an increase in population of 120,601.**

The way I carry out these calculations whilst under timed conditions working with a calculator is as follows:

I firstly input the number 8,000,000 into the calculator by pressing 8, fol-lowed by 'EXP', followed by 6 and finally followed by pressing the 'equals' sign. I can now multiply 8,000,000 by 1.005 and press equals which gives me 8,040,000 which is the population of COUNTRY X after 1 year. Now, to save precious time, I simply multiply 8,040,000 which is currently on the calculator screen by 1.005 again and hit the equals button which gives me 8,080,200. I do the same again and the calculator now displays 8,120,601.

Finally, after multiplying by 1.005 three times, I have found my answer **(a. 3 years)**, because every multiplication by 1.005 means a year's worth of population growth because the 1.005 represents the annual (yearly) pop-ulation growth rate. This is the quickest, most efficient way of solving such a problem.

Although it may seem a long process to arrive at the answer, with practice you will find that it will not take you long to complete. This is because, al-though numerical tests have differing questions they all have a similarity in the method required to solve them. Once you are familiar with the methods required to solve the problems, you are well on your way to scoring 100% on each test taken.

QUESTION 3B

2010 Population Data for Countries X, Y and Z

	POPULATION AT THE BEGINNING OF THE YEAR (millions)	UNEMPLOYMENT RATE (%)	ANNUAL POPULATION GROWTH RATE (%)
COUNTRY X	8	9.5	0.5
COUNTRY Y	9	8.2	0.2
COUNTRY Z	10	7.6	0.8

If both the annual population growth rate and unemployment rate remain the same for all three countries, which country will have the greatest unemployed population by 2013?

a. COUNTRY X
b. COUNTRY Y
c. COUNTRY Z
d. Cannot say

SOLUTION TO QUESTION 3B

To calculate the unemployed population in 2013 for each country, I will need to firstly calculate what the total population of each country will be in 2013.

From part 3a. I know that the population of COUNTRY X at the beginning of 2013 will be 8,120,601.

Knowing that the unemployment rate remains the same no matter how many years have passed, I can use the unemployment rate percentage for COUNTRY X given in the table as 9.5% to calculate the number of unemployed people COUNTRY X contains in 2013 as shown below:

Convert 9.5% into a decimal first:

$$\frac{9.5}{100} = 0.095$$

Now multiply this decimal with the population of COUNTRY X at the beginning of 2013:

$$8,120,601 \times 0.095 = 771457.095$$

COUNTRY X will have 771457.095 unemployed people at the beginning of 2013. I now need to find out how many unemployed people the remaining two countries, Y and Z, will have at the beginning of 2013 in order to compare them and point out which of the three has the greatest unemployed population by 2013.

In order for me to achieve this I will need to firstly calculate the populations of countries Y and Z at the beginning of 2013.

To calculate the population of COUNTRY Y at the beginning of 2013:

1. Convert the annual population growth rate for country Y into a decimal and add 1:

$$1 + (0.2 \div 100) = 1.002$$

In situations such as the above, always calculate what is inside the bracket first, followed by what is outside the bracket. So for the above, 0.2 is divided by 100 first to give 0.002 and then 1 is added to 0.002 to give 1.002

2. Unlike question 3a. where I was not given the number of years to work with, this question clearly tells me to calculate things based on a 3 year period (from 2010 to 2013). There is a useful trick to save time that can be used once the number of years required are known, explained below:

Using the quick method demonstrated in part 3a., I enter 9 million into the calculator display by pressing 9, followed by the 'EXP' button, followed finally by the equals sign. Once this stage is reached it is a matter of multiplying the 9 million by 1.002 (the annual population growth rate) three times, which would look like this:

Population of COUNTRY Y, 2013

$$9,000,000 \times \boxed{1.002 \times 1.002 \times 1.002} = 9,054,108.\ 072$$

$$\downarrow$$

$$(1.002)^3$$

The easier way of doing this is to multiply the 9,000,000 by 1.002 cubed, also known as 1.002 'to the power of 3' and displayed as $(1.002)^3$ which is the same as multiplying out 1.002 three times as shown above. Doing it using the 'cubed' method means less buttons to be pressed on a calculator to find the same answer, which means less time wasted. Simply enter 9 million into the calculator display using the 'EXP' method followed by typing in 1.002 and then pressing the 'x^3' button on your scientific calculator, followed by the equals sign. This will carry out the calculation below:

$$9,000,000 \times (1.002)^3 = 9,054,108.072$$

This is the population of COUNTRY Y at the beginning of 2013. Using this, I can now establish the number of unemployed people COUNTRY Y has in 2013.

The unemployment rate for COUNTRY Y is 8.2% and it stays at 8.2% regardless of how many years pass by as stated in the question. The procedure to calculate the number of unemployed people in COUNTRY Y by 2013 is the same as shown for COUNTRY X:

Start by converting 8.2% into a decimal:

$$\frac{8.2}{100} = 0.082$$

Multiplying this decimal by the population of COUNTRY Y at the beginning of 2013 will give the country Y's 2013 unemployed population:

$$0.082 \times 9,054,108.072 = 742436.8619$$

COUNTRY Y's unemployed population by 2013 is 742436.8619

COUNTRY Z's population at the beginning of 2013 can be found using the same method shown above for countries X and Y:

$$\text{COUNTRY Z's annual population growth rate as a decimal} = \frac{0.8}{100} = 0.008$$

Now remember to add 1 to this decimal in order to get an increase in the population every year, just like I did for countries X and Y above:

$$1 + 0.008 = 1.008$$

The population of COUNTRY Z at the beginning of 2010 was 10 million and the 1.008 is to the power of 3 because I want to know the population of COUNTRY Z in 2013, which is 3 years after the year 2010.

COUNTRY Z's population at the beginning of 2013 $= 10,000,000 \times (1.008)^3$

$$= 10,241,925.12$$

I can now proceed to calculate the COUNTRY Z's 2013 unemployed population. The unemployment rate for country Z is 7.6%:

Converting 7.6% into a decimal first gives: $\dfrac{7.6}{100} = 0.076$

Multiplying 0.076 by COUNTRY Z's population at the beginning of 2013 gives the unemployed population of COUNTRY Z by 2013:

COUNTRY Z's unemployed population, year 2013 $= 0.076 \times 10,241,925.12$

$$= 778,386.3091$$

All 3 of the countries unemployed populations by 2013 are summarised in the table below:

YEAR 2013	UNEMPLOYED POPULATION
COUNTRY X	771,457.095
COUNTRY Y	742,436.8619
COUNTRY Z	778,386.3091

It is clear to see from the table above that COUNTRY Z has the greatest unemployed population by 2013. The answer to question 3b. is therefore **c. COUNTRY Z.**

TIP: *During the actual exam if you are faced with a similar question asking you to compare data, the quickest way to get the answer is to go through the steps I have shown above, using the scientific calculator methods I have presented to you and note down the answers to the individual sections (countries X, Y and Z unemployed populations by 2013 in this example) ready for comparisons once you complete all required calculations. Do not waste valuable time drawing out a neat table as I have done above, simply write the answers down quickly but in a way that is easy for you to compare them at the end.*

QUESTION 3C

2010 Population Data for Countries X, Y and Z

	POPULATION AT THE BEGINNING OF THE YEAR (millions)	UNEMPLOYMENT RATE (%)	ANNUAL POPULATION GROWTH RATE (%)
COUNTRY X	8	9.5	0.5
COUNTRY Y	9	8.2	0.2
COUNTRY Z	10	7.6	0.8

All countries have an unemployment rate which remains the same until 2013, however, the annual population growth rate now remains the same up until 2012 then increases by 0.3% for countries X and Y and decreases by 0.6% for COUNTRY Z in 2013, which country will now have the greatest unemployed population in 2013?

a. COUNTRY X
b. COUNTRY Y
c. COUNTRY Z
d. Cannot say

SOLUTION TO QUESTION 3C

In order to solve this question I must calculate the population increase from 2010 to 2012 for each country first. I will begin with COUNTRY X:

COUNTRY X - 2012 total population

Population after 2 years (2012)= $8,000,000 \times (1.005)^2$

= $8,080,200$

> *1.005 is to the power of 2 to give the population increase after 2 years of the same annual population growth rate.*

TIME SAVING TIP: *The 2012 population for COUNTRY X was previously* calculated in question 3a). It is highly advisable to make a note of such data because in the actual tests it is common for data calculated in a previous part of the question to be required to solve other parts of the question and knowing this can save you valuable time. Below is an example of the notes I would have made during the actual exam. They illustrate what I would have written when doing the calculations for question 3a:

COUNTRY X-

Year 2 population= 8,080,200   Year 3 population= 8,120,601

Writing notes like these will not take long at all but will save you time later on as demonstrated by question 3c) which now requires the 2012 population of COUNTRY X.

Although the year 3 population of COUNTRY X (8,120,601) is not required for part c. it was required for part b. and by writing it like this I already had the answer

The next step is to calculate what the new annual population growth rate is for COUNTRY X. At this point, it is worth calculating what the annual population growth rate will be for all three countries after 2012 because sooner or later it will need to be done anyway.

The question states that after 2012, countries X and Y experience a 0.3% increase in annual population growth rate while COUNTRY Z experiences a 0.6% decrease. The annual population growth rate for each country is shown below both before the changes and after:

	ANNUAL POPULATION GROWTH RATE UP TO AND INCLUDING 2012 (%)	ANNUAL POPULATION GROWTH RATE AFTER THE YEAR 2012 (%)	ANNUAL POPULATION GROWTH RATE AFTER THE YEAR 2012 AS A DECIMAL PLUS 1
COUNTRY X	0.5	0.5+0.3=0.8	$1+\dfrac{0.8}{100}=1.008$
COUNTRY Y	0.2	0.2+0.3=0.5	$1+\dfrac{0.5}{100}=1.005$
COUNTRY Z	0.8	0.8−0.6=0.2	$1+\dfrac{0.2}{100}=1.002$

REMEMBER: To increase any number by a given decimal, always add 1 to that decimal as I have done in the last column of the above table. An example of this is calculating the 2013 population of COUNTRY X, shown below. I need to increase the population of COUNTRY X in 2012 to give the 2013 population by multiplying it with a decimal, the decimal being the annual percentage growth rate after the year 2012.

COUNTRY X- 2013 total population

Population of COUNTRY X after 3 years =
Population of COUNTRY X after 2 years × **1.008**
=8,080,200×1.008
=8,144,841.6

COUNTRY X- 2013 unemployed population

The question states that the unemployment rate remains the same throughout the years. For COUNTRY X the unemployment rate is 9.5% and the calculation is shown below:

Unemployed population of COUNTRY X after 3 years $= \dfrac{9.5}{100}$ x **8,144,841.6**

= 773,759.952

TIME SAVING TIP: *Rather than calculate what 9.5% is as a decimal first and noting this down then re-typing it into a calculator, simply type in 9.5/100 into a calculator, press the '=' button then multiply by 8144841.6 and press the '=' button once again to get the answer of 773,759.952.*

The same sequence of calculations must be carried out for countries Y and Z:

COUNTRY Y- 2012 total population

Population after 2 years (2012)=**9,000,000**×(1.002)²

=9,036,036

COUNTRY Y- 2013 total population

Population of COUNTRY Y after 3 years =
Population of COUNTRY Y after 2 years × **1.005**
=9,036,036 × 1.005
=9,081,216.18

COUNTRY Y- 2013 unemployed population

Unemployed population of COUNTRY Y after 3 years = $\dfrac{8.2}{100}$ x 9,081,216.18

=744,659.7268

COUNTRY Z- 2012 total population

Population after 2 years (2012)=10,000,000×(1.008)²

=10,160,140

COUNTRY Z- 2013 total population

This is where COUNTRY Z differs from the previous calculations for countries X and Y. The question states that after 2012 its annual population growth rate decreases by 0.6% which brings the annual population growth rate to 0.2%.

Population of COUNTRY Z after 3 years=
Population of COUNTRY Z after 2 years ×1.002
=10,160,140×1.002
=10,180,460.28

COUNTRY Z- 2013 unemployed population

Unemployed population of COUNTRY Z after 3 years= $\dfrac{7.6}{100}$ x 10,180,460.28

=773,714.9813

The table below compares the 2013 unemployed population of all three countries:

	2013 UNEMPLOYED POPULATION
COUNTRY X	773,759.952
COUNTRY Y	774,659.7268
COUNTRY Z	773,753.8106

This time, COUNTRY X has the greatest unemployed population and has marginally beaten COUNTRY Z to the title of greatest 2013 unemployed population. The actual difference between COUNTRY X's unemployed 2013 population and that of COUNTRY Z's is only 6.1414.

The answer to question 3c is therefore **a. COUNTRY X**

QUESTION 4
DATA ANALYSIS & RATIOS

QUESTION 4A

The table below shows net migration and live birth rates per 1,000 population for three different towns in the year 2010.

	POPULATION AT THE BEGINNING OF THE YEAR (MILLIONS)	NET MIGRATION RATE PER 1,000 POPULATION (JAN-DEC)	LIVE BIRTH RATE PER 1,000 POPULATION (JAN-DEC)	DEATHS PER 1,000 POPULATION (JAN-DEC)
TOWN A	0.2	2.73	16.2	14.3
TOWN B	0.1	1.65	13.1	11.1
TOWN C	0.6	2.5	9.6	5.6

How many migrants were there in 2010 for town's A and B combined?

a. 711
b. 71.1
c. 7110
d. 6095
e. Cannot Say

SOLUTION TO QUESTION 4A

Town A

For TOWN A, there are 2.73 migrants for every 1000 people that live in TOWN A. This is what is meant by the phrase 'per 1000 population'.

The calculation to find out how many migrants there are in TOWN A according to its population is as follows:

1,000 people in TOWN A means **2.73** migrants

0.2 Million people in TOWN A means **x** migrants

MATHEMATICAL TIP: *0.2 million can also be written as 0.2 x 10^6 because the multiplication by is the same as multiplying the 0.2 by the number 1 million (1,000,000). On a calculator this can be done by typing in 0.2 followed by pressing 'EXP' followed by pressing the number 6.*

I now need to find the value of **x** and this can be achieved by cross multiplication. For clarity of explanation, I have circled and highlighted in gray the numbers that need to be multiplied with each other

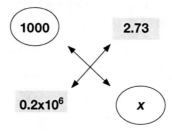

$$1000 \times x = 2.73 \times 0.2 \times 10^6$$

$$1000x = 546000$$

$$x = \frac{546000}{1000} = 546$$

This means that there were **546** migrants in TOWN A during the year 2010.

Town B

TOWN B has 1.65 migrants per 1000 population and has a population of

0.1 million. Using the same method as shown for TOWN A it is possible to find the number of migrants, **y** in TOWN B during the year 2010.

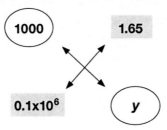

$$1000 \times y = 1.65 \times (0.1 \times 10^6)$$

$$1000y = 165000$$

$$y = \frac{165000}{1000} = 165$$

This means that there were 165 migrants in TOWN A during the year 2010.

To answer question 4a, the number of migrants combined from TOWN A and B during the year 2010 was:

$$546 + 165 = 711$$

The answer to question 4a is **a. 711**

QUESTION 4B

The table below shows net migration and live birth rates per 1,000 population for three different towns in the year 2010.

	POPULATION AT THE BEGINNING OF THE YEAR (MILLIONS)	NET MIGRATION RATE PER 1,000 POPULATION (JAN-DEC)	LIVE BIRTH RATE PER 1,000 POPULATION (JAN-DEC)	DEATHS PER 1,000 POPULATION (JAN-DEC)
TOWN A	0.2	2.73	16.2	14.3
TOWN B	0.1	1.65	13.1	11.1
TOWN C	0.6	2.5	9.6	5.6

How many live births took place in 2010 for TOWN C?

a. 4,553
b. 4,536
c. 5,760
d. 5,766
e. 4,836

SOLUTION TO QUESTION 4B

This question can be solved using the cross multiplication method introduced in the solution to question 4a).

For TOWN C, which has a population of 0.6 million, there are:

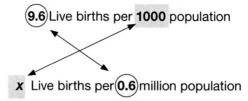

The challenge in this question is finding **x** and this can be achieved using the cross multiplication method:

$$1000 \times x = 9.6 \times (0.6 \times 10^6)$$

$$1000x = 5760000$$

$$x = \frac{5760000}{1000} = 5760$$

The answer to question 4b. is **c. 5760**

QUESTION 4C

The table below shows net migration and live birth rates per 1,000 population for three different towns in the year 2010.

	POPULATION AT THE BEGINNING OF THE YEAR (MILLIONS)	NET MIGRATION RATE PER 1,000 POPULATION (JAN-DEC)	LIVE BIRTH RATE PER 1,000 POPULATION (JAN-DEC)	DEATHS PER 1,000 POPULATION (JAN-DEC)
TOWN A	0.2	2.73	16.2	14.3
TOWN B	0.1	1.65	13.1	11.1
TOWN C	0.6	2.5	9.6	5.6

What was the net effect on the population for town C during 2010 considering live birth and death rates only?

a. +2400
b. -2400
c. +7500
d. -330
e. +750

SOLUTION TO QUESTION 4C

From question 4c., I know that there are 5760 live birth rates in TOWN C for 2010. I now need to calculate the number of deaths, **d** in 2010 for TOWN C. Once again this can be achieved using the cross multiplication method shown in previous parts of question 4.

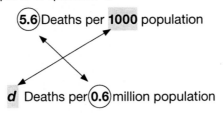

(5.6) Deaths per **1000** population

d Deaths per (0.6) million population

$$1000 \times d = 5.6 \times (0.6 \times 10^6)$$

$$1000d = 3360000$$

$$d = \frac{3360000}{1000} = 3360$$

The number of deaths in 2010 for COUNTRY C was **3360**

To calculate the *net effect* on the population, I need to subtract the live births from the deaths:

Net effect on population in town C, 2010 = 5760 − 3360

= 2400

Because there were more live births than deaths in TOWN C, the net effect was an increase in population, so the answer to question 4c is **a. +2400**

QUESTION 5
DATA ANALYSIS/
COMPARISONS

QUESTION 5A

Weekly vehicle km's for taxi's A and B

TAXI	WEEK 1	WEEK 2	WEEK 3	WEEK 4	WEEK 5
TAXI A	1500	860	2100	1750	1455
TAXI B	2400	3200	1500	4400	3200

If the depreciation costs of the vehicle's per kilometre are £0.60 for TAXI A and £0.50 for TAXI B, what was the difference in depreciation costs between TAXI A and TAXI B in week 2?

a. £ 950
b. £ 1084
c. £ 540
d. £ 2100
e. £ 2995

SOLUTION TO QUESTION 5A

The first thing to do in a situation where there is a table with a heading is to carefully look at the table heading and establish exactly what information the table reveals. So, for question 5a the table reveals the '*weekly* vehicle km's for taxi's A and B' separately. This is important because the question is asking for '*the depreciation costs between TAXI A and TAXI B in* **week 2**'.

Once I know that the column for week 2 shows the total km's driven that week for both taxi's I can answer the question as shown below:

TAXI A depreciation costs are £0.60 and in week 2 taxi A did 860 kilometres (km's).

TAXI A depreciation cost (week 2)= £ 0.60×860

= £ 516

TAXI B depreciation costs are £0.50 and in week 2 taxi B did 3200 kilometres (km's).

TAXI B depreciation cost (week 2)= £ 0.50×3200

= £ 1600

Now that I have both taxi's depreciation costs for week 2 to find the 'difference in depreciation costs between taxi A and taxi B in week 2' simply subtract the lowest depreciation from the highest:

Difference in depreciation (week 2) = £ 1600–£ 516

= £ 1084

The answer to question 5a is therefore **b. £1084**

QUESTION 5B

Weekly vehicle km's for taxi's A and B

TAXI	WEEK 1	WEEK 2	WEEK 3	WEEK 4	WEEK 5
TAXI A	1500	860	2100	1750	1455
TAXI B	2400	3200	1500	4400	3200

The value of TAXI B depreciated in week 4 by £396. If TAXI A's deprecia-tion costs are £0.20 higher per km than TAXI B's in week 4, what were the depreciation costs for TAXI A in week 4?

a. £ 350
b. £ 402.6
c. £ 612
d. £ 507.5
e. £ 455.2

SOLUTION TO QUESTION 5B

TAXI B did 4400 km's in week 4 and depreciated by £396. Because de-preciation occurs per km, it is possible to find out exactly what TAXI B's depreciation cost per km is using the information given in the table and the question as shown below, using the cross multiplication method shown in previous questions:

TAXI B did: **4400 km's and depreciated by £ 396**

Imagine TAXI B did: **1 km and depreciated by £ *x***

To solve the problem I need to find the value of £ *x* and this can be solved through cross multiplication:

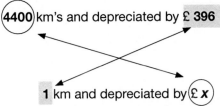

The equation, by multiplying the diagonal opposites above becomes:

$$4400 \times £x = £396 \times 1$$

Rearranging to isolate £ *x* :

$$£ \; x = (£ \; 396 \; ×1) ÷ 4400$$

$$= £ \; 0.09$$

This means that taxi B's depreciation cost per km in week 4 was **£ 0.09**

MATHEMATICAL TIP: *If you didn't already know that 396×1=396 meaning that you can simply type 396÷4400 into a calculator to get the value of x, the above equation is set out with the brackets followed by a division sign. This is exactly how you should type it into your scientific calculator to find the value of x.*

The question now states that the depreciation cost of TAXI A is £0.20 *higher* than TAXI B's per km.

TAXI A's depreciation cost per km=£ 0.09+£ 0.20

=£ 0.29

To calculate the depreciation of TAXI A in week 4, simply multiply TAXI A's depreciation cost per km (£ 0.29) by the total amount of km's driven by TAXI A in week 4, which is 1750 km's from the table.

The amount TAXI A depreciated by in week 4=£0.29×1750

=£ 507.5

The answer to question 5b is **d. £ 507.5**

QUESTION 5C

Weekly vehicle km's for taxi's A and B

TAXI	WEEK 1	WEEK 2	WEEK 3	WEEK 4	WEEK 5
TAXI A	1500	860	2100	1750	1455
TAXI B	2400	3200	1500	4400	3200

Between which two weeks for TAXI A did the lowest percentage change occur in vehicle km's?

a. 1 to 2
b. 2 to 3
c. 3 to 4
d. 4 to 5
e. Cannot Say

SOLUTION TO QUESTION 5C

To solve this question it is necessary to calculate the percentage change between each week for TAXI A only. This can be achieved using the following strategy:

If as is the case between week 1 and week 2 for TAXI A, there is a decrease (numbers changed from 1500 km's in week 1 to 860 km's in week 2) then I use the percentage decrease formula to calculate the percentage change between weeks 1 and 2.

Percentage decrease formula

= [**(highest number - lowest number) ÷ highest number**] × **100%**

On the other hand, if, as is the case between week 2 and week 3, there is an increase in the value of the numbers (changed from 860 in week 2 to 2100 in week 3) I use the percentage increase formula to calculate the percentage change between weeks 2 and 3.

Percentage increase formula

= [**(highest number - lowest number) ÷ lowest number**] × **100%**

TIP TO MEMORISE THE FORMULAS: *Both formulas involve subtracting the highest number from the lowest. If it is the percentage decrease formula* *you require, then remember to divide by the opposite of what a decrease leads to and that is the highest number. If you require the percentage increase formula then remember to divide by the opposite of what an increase leads to which is the lowest number.*

With the strategy explained it is now possible to calculate the percentage change between each week for TAXI A only:

Week 1 to Week 2:

Highest number: 1500 (week 1)

Lowest number: 860 (week 2)

As discussed above, this requires the percentage decrease formula:

% change (week 1 to 2)
= *[(highest number-lowest number)÷highest number]×100%*
= *[(1500−860)÷1500]×100%*
= **42.67%**

Week 2 to week 3:

Highest number: 2100 (week 3)

Lowest number: 860 (week 2)

As discussed above, this requires the percentage increase formula:

% change (week 2 to 3)
= *[(highest number - lowest number)÷lowest number] × 100%*
= *[(2100−860)÷860]×100%*
=**144.19%**

Week 3 to week 4:

Highest number: 2100 (week 3)

Lowest number: 1750 (week 4)

As there has been a decrease between week 3 and 4 I will need to use the percentage decrease formula.

% change (week 3 to 4)
= *[(highest number-lowest number)÷highest number]×100%*
= *[(2100−1750)÷2100]×100%*
= **16.67%**

Week 4 to week 5:

Highest number: 1750 (week 4)

Lowest number: 1455 (week 5)

As there has been a decrease between week 4 and 5 I will need to use the percentage decrease formula.

% change (week 4 to 5)

$= [(highest\ number - lowest\ number) \div highest\ number] \times 100\%$
$= [(1750 - 1455) \div 1750] \times 100\%$
$= \mathbf{16.86\%}$

The question is asking for the lowest percentage change that occurred between two weeks in vehicle km's, the summary table below helps find the lowest percentage change:

Summary table:

WEEKS	1 TO 2	2 TO 3	3 TO 4	4 TO 5
% CHANGE	42.67%	144.19 %	16.67%	16.86%

The lowest percentage change that occurred is between week 3 and week 4.

The answer to question 5c is **c. '3 to 4'**

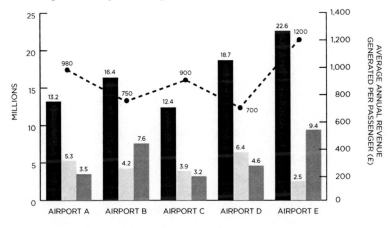

QUESTION 6
DATA INTERPRETATION, ANALYSIS & RATIO

QUESTION 6A

Passenger data for the year 2010

Business passengers (millions)

Economy passengers (millions)

Number of Flights (millions)

- - - - Average Annual Revenue Generated per Passenger (£)

Taking into account the total annual revenue generated per airport, what is the revenue difference in millions, between the airport which generates the lowest total annual revenue and the airport with the largest total annual revenue?

a. £7,890

b. £6,557

c. £7,980

d. £7,700

e. £ 6,990

SOLUTION TO QUESTION 6A

The graph contains information on the average annual revenue generated per passenger. So, for example a passenger who uses airport A pays on average £980 per year.

The graph also contains information on how many passengers have used a particular airport in the year 2010. To find the total amount of passengers who have used a particular airport during the year 2010, simply add the amount of business class and economy class passengers together.

Once the total number of passengers using a particular airport has been established, then it is a matter of multiplying this by the average annual revenue generated per passenger which will reveal the total annual airport revenue. If this procedure is repeated for all airports, it is possible to isolate the two airports containing both the highest total annual revenue and the lowest and then subtract them to reveal the revenue difference, which is what the question is asking for.

The entire procedure is shown below:

Airport A
Total passengers=Economy passengers+Business passengers

$$= 5.3 \text{ million}+3.5 \text{ million}$$

$$= \textbf{8.8 } \textit{million}$$

Average Annual Revenue generated per passenger = £ 980

Annual Revenue generated at AIRPORT A = £ 980 × 8.8 million

$$= \textbf{£ 8,624 } \textit{million}$$

 THE **TESTING** SERIES

TIME SAVING TIP: *Rather than use 5300000+3500000 = 8800000 it is much easier to use the form:*

$$5.3 \text{ million} + 3.5 \text{ million} = 8.8 \text{ million}$$

The only difference between the two is that one contains the word 'million' which represents the same thing as actually writing out the number in full. This saves possible errors occurring and also means you have less to type into a calculator which will save time in the exam.

Airport B

Total passengers=Economy passengers+Business passengers

=7.6 million+4.2 million

=11.8 million

Average Annual Revenue generated per passenger = £ 750

Annual Revenue generated at AIRPORT A = £ 750×11.8 million

= £ 8,850 *million*

Airport C

Total passengers=Economy passengers+Business passengers

=3.2 million+3.9 million

=7.1 *million*

Average Annual Revenue generated per passenger= £ 900

Annual Revenue generated at AIRPORT A= £ 900×7.1 million

= £ 6,390 *million*

Airport D

Total passengers=Economy passengers+Business passengers

=4.6 million+6.4 million

=11 *million*

Average Annual Revenue generated per passenger = £ 980

Annual Revenue generated at AIRPORT A = £ 700×11 million

= £ 7,700

Airport E

Total passengers= Economy passengers+Business passengers

$$= 9.4 \text{ million} + 2.5 \text{ million}$$

$$= \textbf{11.9 million}$$

Average Annual Revenue generated per passenger = £ 1200

Annual Revenue generated at AIRPORT A = £ 1200×11.9 million

$$= \textbf{£ 14,280 million}$$

Summary table

AIRPORT	AIRPORT A	AIRPORT B	AIRPORT C	AIRPORT D	AIRPORT E
ANNUAL REVENUE (millions)	£ 8,624	£ 8,850	£ 6,390	£ 7,700	£ 14,280

From the calculations, it can be seen that Airport C has generated the lowest total revenue in the year 2010 and Airport E has generated the highest total revenue during the year 2010.

The next step is to subtract the highest total revenue from the lowest total revenue:

Revenue difference =£ 14,280 million−£ 6,390 million

$$= \textbf{£ 7,890}$$

TOP TIP: *Can you now see that even if you failed to spot the fact that passenger numbers were in millions it wouldn't have any significance on your final answer? The word 'million' has simply come along for the ride and if you really wanted to save time and saw this coming you could ignore the fact that passenger numbers were in millions and do the calculations as if they were not in millions to get exactly the same answer! This would save a significant amount of time in the exam.*

The answer to question 6a is **a. £7,890**

QUESTION 6B

Passenger data for the year 2010

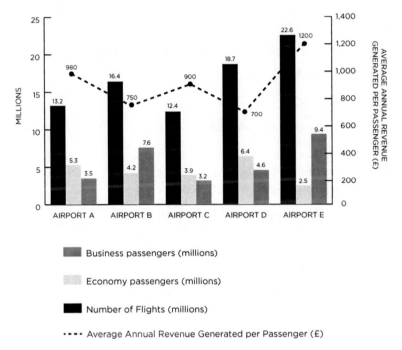

Business passengers (millions)

Economy passengers (millions)

Number of Flights (millions)

- - - - Average Annual Revenue Generated per Passenger (£)

Which airport has the greatest number of flights per passenger (economy and business)?

a. Airport A
b. Airport B
c. Airport C
d. Airport D
e. Airport E

SOLUTION TO QUESTION 6B

NOTE: Another way of asking this question is "Which airport has the greatest number of flight to passenger (economy and business) ratio". Question 6c) explains the method of solving such questions in detail using a slightly different method to the one given to solve question 6b) below.

The method for solving this question is to find from the graph the number of flights that took place for all passengers and then proceed to calculate the number of flights that took place 'per passenger'. The procedure for doing this is given below:

Airport A

Total passengers = Economy passengers + Business passengers

= 5.3 million + 3.5 million

= 8.8 million

Number of flights that took place with 8.8 million passengers = 13.2 million *(from chart)*

I now need to find the number of flights that took place with 1 passenger. This can be achieved using cross multiplication:

With **8.8 million** passengers there are **13.2 million** flights

With **1** passenger there are **a** flights

The value of **a** needs to be found:

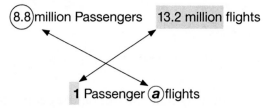

The equation then becomes:

$$8.8 \text{ million} \times a = 13.2 \text{ million} \times 1$$

Rearranging to find:

$$a = \frac{13.2 \text{ million} \times 1}{8.8 \text{ million}}$$

NOTE: The word 'million' cancels out from the numerator and denominator of the fraction above, so writing out the full number, for example, 13.2 million as 13200000 means spending time figuring out how many zeros need to be included and then typing it all into your calculator which is a complete waste of precious exam time. It is much neater and quicker to do it the way I have as above, which will leave you with a simple calculation to solve as shown below:

$$a = \frac{13.2}{8.8} = 1.5$$

Therefore, AIRPORT A has 1.5 flights per passenger.

To answer question 6b, I must now do the same for all airports in order to discover which airport has the 'greatest number of flights per passenger'.

Airport B

Total passengers = Economy passengers + Business passengers

=7.6 million+4.2 million

=11.8 million

Number of flights that took place with 11.8 million passengers =16.4 million *(from chart)*

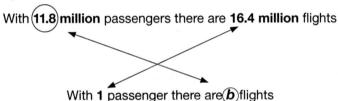

With **11.8 million** passengers there are **16.4 million** flights

With **1** passenger there are **b** flights

Creating an equation to find the value of **b**:

11.8 million×b=16.4 million×1

Rearranging to find :
$$b = \frac{16.4 \ \text{million} \times 1}{11.8 \ \text{million}}$$

$$b = \frac{16.4}{11.8} = 1.39$$

Therefore, AIRPORT B has 1.39 flights per passenger.

Airport C

Total passengers = Economy passengers + Business passengers

=3.2 million+3.9 million

=7.1 million

Number of flights that took place with 7.1 million passengers =12.4 million *(from chart)*

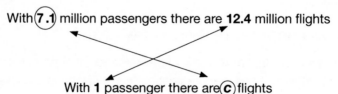

With (7.1) million passengers there are **12.4** million flights

With **1** passenger there are (c) flights

Creating an equation to find the value of **c**:

$$\textbf{7.1 million} \times \textbf{c} = \textbf{12.4 million} \times \textbf{1}$$

Rearranging to find **c**:

$$c = \frac{12.4 \text{ million} \times 1}{7.1 \text{ million}}$$

$$c = \frac{12.4}{7.1} = 1.75$$

Therefore, AIRPORT C has 1.75 flights per passenger.

Airport D

Total passengers = Economy passengers + Business passengers

=4.6 million+6.4 million

= 11 million

Number of flights that took place with 11 million passengers =18.7 million *(from chart)*

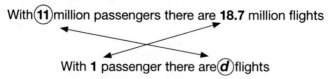

With (11) million passengers there are **18.7** million flights

With **1** passenger there are (d) flights

Creating an equation to find the value of **d**:

$$\textbf{11 million} \times \textbf{d} = \textbf{18.7 million} \times \textbf{1}$$

Rearranging to find **d**:

$$d = \frac{18.7 \text{ million} \times 1}{11 \text{ million}}$$

$$d = \frac{18.7}{11} = 1.7$$

Therefore, AIRPORT D has 1.7 flights per passenger.

Airport E

Total passengers = Economy passengers + Business passengers

=9.4 million+2.5 million

= 11.9 million

Number of flights that took place with 11.9 million passengers =22.6 million *(from chart)*

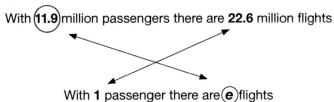

With (**11.9**) million passengers there are **22.6** million flights

With **1** passenger there are (**e**) flights

Creating an equation to find the value of **e**:

11.9 million × e = 22.6 million × 1

Rearranging to find **e** :

$$e = \frac{22.6 \text{ million} \times 1}{11.9 \text{ million}}$$

$$e = \frac{22.6}{11.9} = 1.90$$

Therefore, AIRPORT E has 1.90 flights per passenger.

Summary table:

AIRPORT	AIRPORT A	AIRPORT B	AIRPORT C	AIRPORT D	AIRPORT E
NUMBER OF FLIGHTS PER PASSENGER (MILLIONS)	1.5	1.39	1.75	1.7	1.90

It is now easy to see that Airport E has the greatest number of flights per passenger.

The answer to question 6b is **e. Airport E**

QUESTION 6C

Passenger data for the year 2010

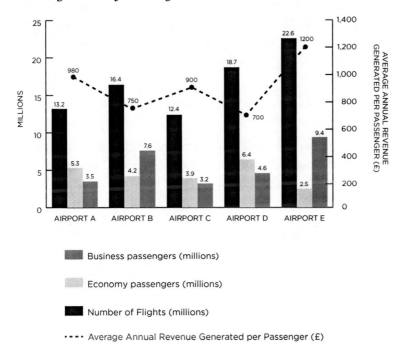

    Business passengers (millions)

    Economy passengers (millions)

    Number of Flights (millions)

- - - - Average Annual Revenue Generated per Passenger (£)

Which airport has the greatest ratio of economy passengers to that of business passengers?

a. Airport A
b. Airport B
c. Airport C
d. Airport D
e. Airport E

SOLUTION TO QUESTION 6C

Another way of asking this question could be: *"Which airport has the greatest number of economy passengers per business passenger?"* Therefore, if you have understood the method of question 6b) you can use it to solve this question. However, I would like to introduce you to a quicker way of solving questions involving ratios.

Ratios

The result of a ratio shows the value of one quantity in comparison to another. So, for example, if there is a bag containing 3 sweets in total and 2 of the sweets are red with the remaining sweet green, it can be said that the ratio of red sweets to green sweets is 2 i.e. there are 2 red sweets for every green sweet. The calculation would be as follows:

$$\text{Ratio of red sweets to green sweets} = \frac{2}{1} = 2$$

To solve this question, the ratio Economy class passengers to business class passengers will need to be calculated for every airport using the same principles and the method is given below.

Airport A

Economy passengers = 5.3 million

$$\text{Ratio} = \frac{5.3 \text{ million}}{3.5 \text{ million}} = \frac{5.3}{3.5} = 1.51$$

Business passengers = 3.5 million

AIRPORT A's ratio of economy class passengers to that of business class passengers is **1.5**.

Note that the ratio is economy class passengers TO business class passengers and not the other way around. It is important to remain consistent and ensure that all further calculations are done using the method shown above i.e. economy passengers divided by business passengers.

Airport B

Economy passengers = 4.2 million

$$\text{Ratio} = \frac{4.2 \text{ million}}{7.6 \text{ million}} = \frac{4.2}{7.6} = 0.55$$

Business passengers = 7.6 million

AIRPORT B's ratio of economy class passengers to that of business class passengers is **0.55**.

Airport C

Economy passengers = 3.9 million

$$\text{Ratio} = \frac{3.9 \text{ million}}{3.2 \text{ million}} = \frac{3.9}{3.2} = 1.22$$

Business passengers = 3.2 million

AIRPORT C's ratio of economy class passengers to that of business class passengers is **1.22**.

Airport D

Economy passengers = 6.4 million

$$\text{Ratio} = \frac{6.4 \text{ million}}{4.6 \text{ million}} = \frac{6.4}{4.6} = 1.39$$

Business passengers = 4.6 million

AIRPORT D's ratio of economy class passengers to that of business class passengers is **1.39**.

Airport E

Economy passengers = 2.5 million

$$\text{Ratio} = \frac{2.5 \text{ million}}{9.4 \text{ million}} = \frac{2.5}{9.4} = 0.27$$

Business passengers = 9.4 million

AIRPORT E's ratio of economy class passengers to that of business class passengers is **0.27**.

Summary table:

AIRPORT	AIRPORT A	AIRPORT B	AIRPORT C	AIRPORT D	AIRPORT E
RATIO OF ECONOMY CLASS PASSENGERS TO BUSINESS CLASS PASSENGERS	1.51	0.55	1.22	1.39	0.27

AIRPORT A has the greatest ratio of economy class passengers to business class passengers which makes the answer to question 6c
a. AIRPORT A

QUESTION 7
RATIO AND EXCHANGE RATE

QUESTION 7A

Orders placed with business supplies UK

UNIT ORDER	BOOKS	STATIONERY	MACHINERY
S.M BOOKS & OFFICE SUPPLIES	17,500	6,500	0
MANUFACTURING INC.	0	3,200	12,300
J.H BOOK PRINTERS & SELLERS	20	7,800	4,200
PRICE PER UNIT (£)	£3	£12	£560

Exchange rates for Sterling (£)

VALUE OF £1 IN EURO AND US DOLLARS.	EURO	US DOLLAR
1ST JANUARY	1.25	1.80
1ST JULY	1.30	1.90

If you changed 330 US Dollars into Euros on 1st July, how many Euros would you receive?

a. 329.45

b. 225.79

c. 338.65

d. 145.55

e. 233.05

SOLUTION TO QUESTION 7A

This question may appear tricky to you in the first instance as there is no direct relationship between Dollars and Euros. However, this can be easily solved.

The table shows the value of £1 in both Euros and US dollars on 1st July.

On the 1st July, £1 was worth 1.30 in Euros and 1.90 in dollars.

If £1 is 1.30 EUR and also $1.90, then it follows that 1.30 EUR must have the same value as $1.90.

I have now established a direct relationship between Euros and Dollars. This will allow me to convert 330 US Dollar into Euros using the 1st July exchange.

1.90 Dollars is equivalent to 1.30 Euros, so how many Euros would 330 dollars be worth? The answer can be found by creating an equation as shown and solving for x:

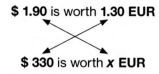

$ 1.90 is worth **1.30 EUR**

$ 330 is worth x **EUR**

Creating an equation to find the value of x Euros:

$$1.90 \times x = 330 \times 1.30$$

$$x = \frac{330 \times 1.3}{1.90} = 225.79 \text{ Euros}$$

The answer to question 7a is b. 225.79 Euros

QUESTION 7B

Orders placed with business supplies UK

UNIT ORDER	BOOKS	STATIONERY	MACHINERY
S.M BOOKS & OFFICE SUPPLIES	17,500	6,500	0
MANUFACTURING INC.	0	3,200	12,300
J.H BOOK PRINTERS & SELLERS	20	7,800	4,200
PRICE PER UNIT (£)	£3	£12	£560

Exchange rates for Sterling (£)

VALUE OF £1 IN EURO AND US DOLLARS.	EURO	US DOLLAR
1ST JANUARY	1.25	1.80
1ST JULY	1.30	1.90

The price of books per unit increases by £0.25, what is the percentage increase on the cost of the S.M books & office supplies' order?

a. 0.55%
b. 6.25%
c. 33.3%
d. 8.33%
e. 7.49%

SOLUTION TO QUESTION 7B

The formula for percentage increase was given in the solution to question 5c and is provided again below for your reference. The first formula is for general use and the second is specifically tailored to this question:

Percentage increase formula

= [(*highest number - lowest number*) ÷ *lowest number*] × 100%

Percentage increase formula for this particular question:

=[(*highest cost order-lowest cost order*)÷*lowest cost order*] × 100%

For this particular question the 'lowest number' refers to the 'lowest cost' of the S.M books & office supplies' order and the 'highest number' refers to the 'highest cost' of the S.M books & office supplies' order.

To obtain the 'lowest cost order' I must use the price per unit of £3 for books before it increased by £0.25.

S.M books & office supplies order 17,500 books (from the table). At £3 per book, this equates to:

$$17,500 × £3 = £52,500$$

£52,500 is the *'lowest cost order'* and I now need to find what the 'highest cost order' is.

As the price of book per unit has increased by £0.25, the new price per unit is £3.25.

S.M books & office supplies order 17,500 books (from the table). At £3.25 per book, this equates to:

$$17,500 × £3.25 = £56,875$$

£56,875 is the *'highest cost order'*. I now have all the values required to find the percentage increase on the cost of the S.M books & office supplies' order. Referring back to the percentage increase formula for this question:

% increase=[(*highest cost order-lowest cost order*)÷*lowest cost order*] × 100%

$$=£56,875 - £52,500 ÷ £52,500 × 100\%$$

$$=4375 ÷ 52,500 × 100\%$$

$$=0.0833 × 100\%$$

$$=8.33\%$$

The answer to question 7b is d. 8.33%

QUESTION 7C

Orders placed with business supplies UK

UNIT ORDER	BOOKS	STATIONERY	MACHINERY
S.M BOOKS & OFFICE SUPPLIES	17,500	6,500	0
MANUFACTURING INC.	0	3,200	12,300
J.H BOOK PRINTERS & SELLERS	20	7,800	4,200
PRICE PER UNIT (£)	£3	£12	£560

Exchange rates for Sterling (£)

VALUE OF £1 IN EURO AND US DOLLARS.	EURO	US DOLLAR
1ST JANUARY	1.25	1.80
1ST JULY	1.30	1.90

Assuming Manufacturing inc. places orders for the same number of unit's of Stationery in both January and July and confirms the order price in £ Sterling, what would the cost difference be in Euros if the order was paid for on the 1st January rather than on the 1st July?

a. 1,920 EUR More
b. 2,995 EUR Less
c. 2,995 EUR More
d. 1,920 EUR Less
e. 3,300 EUR More

SOLUTION TO QUESTION 7C

Between 1st January and 1st July, the price per unit for stationery has remained the same at £12.

Manufacturing inc. orders 3,200 unit's of stationery at £12 each which equates to:

$$3200 \times £12 = £38,400$$

Assuming manufacturing inc. paid in sterling, £ 38,400 is the price they would have paid for 3,200 units of stationery on both 1st January and 1st July. However, the question is asking for the difference in price in Euros for both dates and converting Sterling to Euros involves exchange rates, which is what causes a difference in price for the two dates. In the explanation below, **Y** EUR is the price Manufacturing inc. paid in Euros for 3,200 units of stationery on 1st January.

On 1st January, £1 was worth 1.25 EUR which means,

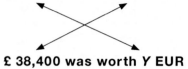

£ 38,400 was worth Y EUR

I must now create an equation and solve it to find the value of Y:

TIME SAVING TIP: *If you can see that by multiplying £38,400 with 1.25 EUR, which acts as a conversion factor for converting sterling into Euro will give you the answer in Euros, congratulations, you will not have to create an equation and solve it. If you can't see it yet, then through practice you will eventually instinctively know when faced with similar situations, that multiplying by the conversion factor is the quickest way of solving such a problem.*

$$1 \times Y = 38{,}400 \times 1.25$$

$$Y = 48{,}000 \text{ EUR}$$

On the 1st January, Manufacturing inc. paid **48,000** Euros for 3,200 units of stationery.

To complete the solution to the question, I now need to calculate the price paid in Euros by Manufacturing inc. on 1st July for 3,200 units of stationery. From the table, I can see that on 1st July £1 is worth 1.30 EUR. Let **z** be the price paid for 3,200 units of stationery by Manufacturing inc. in Euros on 1st July.

On 1st July, £1 was worth 1.30 EUR which means,

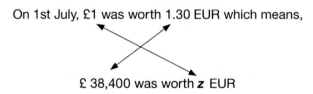

£ 38,400 was worth z EUR

I must now create an equation and solve it to find the value of z:

$$1 \times z = 38,400 \times 1.30$$

$$z = 49,920 \text{ EUR}$$

On the 1st July, Manufacturing inc. paid **49,920** Euros for 3,200 units of stationery.

The final part of the question asks: *"What would be the cost difference in Euro's if the order was paid for on the 1st January rather than on the 1st July?"*

There are two things to do here. Firstly, I need to calculate the cost difference which can be found by subtracting the two prices:

$$\textbf{Cost difference} = 49,920 \text{ EUR} - 48,000 \text{ EUR}$$
$$= 1,920 \text{ EUR}$$

Secondly and finally, I need to decide if the answer is 1,920 EUR more or 1,920 EUR less. This can be deduced from the wording of the question which asks for the cost difference if the order was paid on 1st January rather than 1st July. Because the price in Euros on 1st January (48,000 EUR) was less than the price on 1st July (49,920 EUR), a saving of 1,920 EUR has been made and therefore by paying on 1st January rather than 1st July, Manufacturing inc. are paying 1,920 EUR Less.

The answer to question 7c is d. 1,920 EUR Less

QUESTION 8
PIE CHART AND PERCENTAGE

QUESTION 8A

C.T. METALS - METAL ORDERS BREAKDOWN FOR LAST YEAR

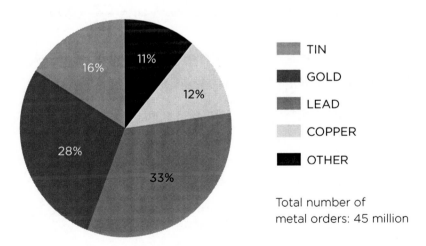

11%

12%

16%

28%

33%

■ TIN
■ GOLD
■ LEAD
■ COPPER
■ OTHER

Total number of
metal orders: 45 million

What was the total number of Copper and Tin ordered combined?

a. 12.6 million

b. 13.2 million

c. 22 million

d. 14.6 million

e. Cannot say

SOLUTION TO QUESTION 8A

There are two methods of solving this question; you may select the one you prefer to use. Both are equally as good although method 2 may lead to the answer quicker, depending on how quickly you can analyse the data and type into a calculator.

TIP: *When typing in 45 million into a calculator, type in 45 followed by the 'EXP' button followed by the number 6 followed by the equals sign. Doing this is equivalent to typing in 45,000,000 into a calculator screen but much faster and always accurate.*

Method 1

The total number of metal orders was 45 million last year. 12% of these orders were copper and 16% were tin.

Copper orders as a decimal of the total orders last year = $\dfrac{12}{100} = 0.12$

Number of Copper orders last year = $0.12 \times 45 \times 10^6 = 5,400,000$ (5.4 million)

To calculate the above, I simply typed into my calculator the following in order:

0.12

×

45

EXP

6

=

This gave me 5400000 on my calculator screen which is 5.4 million. This means that copper orders were 5.4 million last year.

TIP: *When there is a large number on the calculator screen such as 5400000 and you want to know where to place the decimal so you can shorten the number and call it 'million', for example 5400000 becomes 5.4 million then either write the number down accurately on a paper and count back six decimal places as shown:*

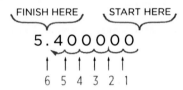

Or, alternatively, using a calculator, you can press the button containing an arrow above it which, when pressed with 5400000 on the calculator display will show 5.4×10^6 which indicates that it is 5.4 million. On my casio fx-85 calculator, the arrow I am referring to is located above a button which has 'ENG' written on it.

Have a play around with your calculator to find this button as it will save you time compared to having to do it the alternative method shown above. Note that once you have located the button with an arrow, you may have to press the 'shift' button first before using the arrow key.

Now try calculating the number of tin orders using your calculator:

Tin orders as a decimal of the total orders last year = $\dfrac{16}{100}$ = 0.16

Number of Copper orders last year = $0.16 \times 45 \times 10^6$ = 7,200,000 (7.2 million)

There were 7.2 million Tin orders last year.

The question asks for *"the total number of Copper and Tin ordered combined"*:

Copper and Tin orders combined = 5.4 million + 7.2 million

= 12.6 million

Method 2

Add the two percentages together:

Copper orders 12%

Tin orders 16%

Copper and Tin orders combined in percent $= 12\% + 16\% = 28\%$

Now calculate how many orders 28% accounts for out of the 45 million orders that took place last year:

As a decimal of the total orders last year, $28\% = \dfrac{28}{100} = 0.28$

Copper and Tin orders combined $= 0.28 \times 45 \times 10^6 = 12,600,000$ (12.6 million)

The answer to question 8a is **a. 12.6 million**

QUESTION 8B

C.T. METALS - METAL ORDERS BREAKDOWN FOR LAST YEAR

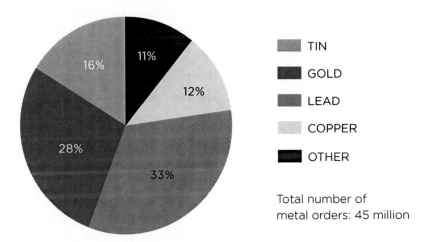

Total number of
metal orders: 45 million

How many more Lead orders took place compared to Gold orders last year?

a. 1,599,765
b. 2,250,000
c. 3,555,375
d. 22,555,212
e. 41,340,192

SOLUTION TO QUESTION 8B

This question is different to the previous question as it is asking for the difference between Lead orders and Gold orders rather than the combined order which means that method 2 of question 8a. cannot be used here.

To find the solution, the number of lead orders last year will need to be calculated followed by the calculation of the number of gold orders last year separately, which is similar to method 1 in question 8a. and subtracting them will give the answer. The method is shown below:

The total number of metal orders was 45 million last year. 33% of these orders were lead and 28% were gold.

Lead orders as a decimal of the total orders last year $= \dfrac{33}{100} = 0.33$

Number of Lead orders last year $= 0.33 \times 45 \times 10^6 = \mathbf{14{,}850{,}000}$ (14.85 million)

There were 14.85 million lead orders last year.

Gold Orders as a decimal of the total orders last year $= \dfrac{28}{100} = 0.28$

Number of Lead orders last year $= 0.28 \times 45 \times 10^6 = \mathbf{12{,}600{,}000}$ (12.6 million)

There were 12.6 million Gold orders last year.

To find how many more Lead orders took place compared to Gold orders last year I need to now find the difference in the number of orders by subtracting:

Difference = 14,850,000 − 12,600,000

= 2,250,000

Because the number of Lead orders was higher than Gold orders last year, it can be said that there were 2,250,000 more orders for Lead than Gold last year.

The answer to question 8b. is **b. 2,250,000**

TIP: *Notice how I carried out the 'difference' calculation. I took into consideration that the multiple choice answers to this question were in the form 2,250,000 rather than 2.25 million which led me to calculate the difference using the form*

Difference = 14,850,000 − 12,600,000

Rather than:

Difference = 14.85 million − 12.6 million

If the multiple answers were in the form 2.25 million as was the case in question 8a I would have used the latter format.

QUESTION 8C

C.T. METALS - METAL ORDERS BREAKDOWN FOR LAST YEAR

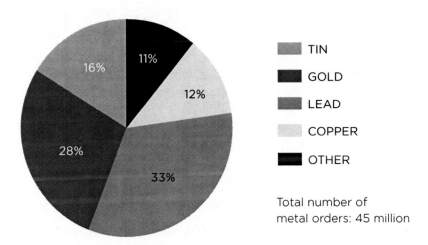

TIN

GOLD

LEAD

COPPER

OTHER

Total number of
metal orders: 45 million

If the total income generated from Copper for C.T. Metals was £250 million, approximately how much income would be generated per order of copper?

a. £39.30
b. £46.30
c. £25.45
d. £52.50
e. £29.40

SOLUTION TO QUESTION 8C

The first step to take towards solving this question would be to either refer to the notes made from question 8a) where a calculation of the number of copper orders last year was necessary or alternatively, if no notes were made, you would have to quickly calculate the total number of copper orders last year using method 1 from question 8a shown again below:

The total number of metal orders was 45 million last year. 12% of these orders were copper.

Copper orders as a decimal of the total orders last year = $\dfrac{12}{100} = 0.12$

Number of Copper orders last year = $0.12 \times 45 \times 10^6 = 5,400,000$ (5.4 million)

The question states that the total number of copper orders last year, which amounted to 5.4 million orders, generated an income for C.T metals worth £250 million. I now need to find the value per order of Copper. The method for doing this is shown below:

5.4 million Orders of Copper was worth £250 million which means,

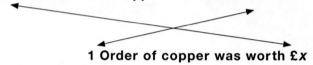

1 Order of copper was worth £x

Cross multiplying gives the following equation which will enable me to find the amount of income generated on each order of Copper last year for C.T metals:

$$5.4 \text{ million} \times £x = £250 \text{ million} \times 1$$

$$£x = (£250 \text{ million} \times 1) \div 5.4 \text{ million}$$

$$£x = £250 \text{ million} \div 5.4$$

$$£x = £46.296 \text{ (approximately £46.30 when rounded up)}$$

This means that the income generated per order of Copper for C.T Metals was approximately £46.30 last year. The answer to question 8c is therefore **b. £46.30**

QUESTION 9
DATA INTERPRETATION AND PERCENTAGE

QUESTION 9A

Percentage of total staff at XYZ Company (Staff Distribution)

FUNCTION	HR	FINANCE	SALES	DISTRIBUTION	OTHER	TOTAL
YEAR 1	22	7	33	24	14	100
YEAR 2	35	7	25	16	17	100
YEAR 3	24	9	29	18	20	100
YEAR 4	18	8	32	15	27	100
YEAR 5	15	10	41	18	16	100

In YEAR 2 there were 502 people employed in sales. How many people in total were employed by XYZ Company in YEAR 2?

a. 3667
b. 1547
c. 6994
d. 2008
e. 2034

SOLUTION TO QUESTION 9A

The question tells me that in year 2, 502 people were employed in sales in YEAR 2. From the table, this accounts for 25% of all people employed by XYZ Company in YEAR 2.

The question that should be raised at this point is: *"If 502 people account for 25% of all people employed in year 2 by XYZ Company, how many people would account for 100%?"*

There are two methods of answering this.

Method 1

If you know that 25% is ¼ of 100% i.e. four times less than 100%, then it follows that 25% multiplied by 4 will equal 100%. Therefore, the 502 people that account for 25% of all employed people in year 2 can be multiplied by 4 to get the total number of employees in YEAR 2 (100% of employees):

Total number of employees in year 2 employed by XYZ Company=502×4

=2008 employees

Method 2

502 People accounts for 25% of total employees in YEAR 2 at XYZ Company

***x* People account for 100% of total employees in YEAR 2 at XYZ Company**

Cross multiplying gives the following equation, which will allow me to find the quantity x :

$$x \times 25\% = 502 \times 100\%$$

$$X = \frac{502 \times 100\%}{25\%}$$

NOTE: At this stage, it is not necessary to convert the percentages into decimals because 100% divided by 25% equals 4, so the two cancel out as shown below:

$$X = \frac{502 \times 100\%_{(4)}}{25\%_{(1)}} = \frac{502 \times 4}{1} = 502 \times 4 = 2008 \text{ employees}$$

The answer to question 9a is **d. 2008 employees** were employed in total by XYZ Company in YEAR 2.

QUESTION 9B

Percentage of total staff at XYZ Company (Staff Distribution)

FUNCTION	HR	FINANCE	SALES	DISTRIBUTION	OTHER	TOTAL
YEAR 1	22	7	33	24	14	100
YEAR 2	35	7	25	16	17	100
YEAR 3	24	9	29	18	20	100
YEAR 4	18	8	32	15	27	100
YEAR 5	15	10	41	18	16	100

If the number of staff working in finance in YEAR 3 was the same as the number of staff working in finance in YEAR 4 and 2,400 people were employed at XYZ Company in YEAR 3, how many employees were there at XYZ Company in YEAR 4?

a. 3695
b. 4334
c. 2321
d. 2700
e. 1985

SOLUTION TO QUESTION 9B

First, I examine the first statement made in the question:

"If the number of staff working in finance in YEAR 3 was the same as the number of staff working in finance in YEAR 4…"

The table gives percentages of staff working in finance.

9% of total employees in YEAR 3 work in the finance function

8% of total employees in YEAR 4 work in the finance function

From the first part of the question (statement above), these are equal to each other:

8% of total employees in YEAR 4=9% of total employees in YEAR 3

The next part of the question states *"…2,400 people were employed at XYZ Company in YEAR 3, how many employees were there at XYZ Company in YEAR 4?"*

From this part of the question I can deduce that the total number of employees in YEAR 3 was 2,400. The final part of the question asks how many employees were working at XYZ Company in YEAR 4.

Referring back to the equation which derived from the first part of the question, there is now only one unknown to find, the total employees in YEAR 4:

9% of total employees in YEAR 3 =8% of total employees in YEAR 4

TIP: *In mathematics, the word 'of' means multiply. Therefore, the equation now becomes:*

$$8\% \times \textit{total employees in year 4}=9\% \times \textit{total employees in year 3}$$

Rearranging the equation to isolate 'total employees in year 4' gives:

Total employees in YEAR 4=(9%×total employees in YEAR 3)÷8%

Total employees in YEAR 4=(9/100×2400)÷8/100

Total employees in YEAR 4=(0.09×2400)÷0.08

Total employees in YEAR 4=2700

The answer to question **9b is d. 2700 employees** in total were working at XYZ Company in YEAR 4.

QUESTION 9C

Percentage of total staff at XYZ Company (Staff Distribution)

FUNCTION	HR	FINANCE	SALES	DISTRIBUTION	OTHER	TOTAL
YEAR 1	22	7	33	24	14	100
YEAR 2	35	7	25	16	17	100
YEAR 3	24	9	29	18	20	100
YEAR 4	18	8	32	15	27	100
YEAR 5	15	10	41	18	16	100

Between which two years did the number of staff in HR change the most?

a. YEAR 1 – YEAR 2
b. YEAR 2 – YEAR 3
c. YEAR 3 – YEAR 4
d. YEAR 4 – YEAR 5
e. Cannot Say

SOLUTION TO QUESTION 9C

To answer this question I will need to find the two years that produced the largest difference in numbers of HR staff. The two years which had the largest difference in HR staff in comparison to the other years is the one where the number of staff in HR changed the most.

There is, however, a slight problem in finding which two years had the largest difference in HR staff. No data is given on how many HR staff there actually were, only the percentage of HR staff working every year. Without knowing the total number of staff working in each year, it is impossible to answer this question.

Question 9d has been included below to deal with a situation where such data is provided.

The answer to question 9c is therefore **e. 'Cannot Say'**

QUESTION 9D

Percentage of total staff at XYZ Company (Staff Distribution)

FUNCTION	HR	FINANCE	SALES	DISTRIBUTION	OTHER	TOTAL
YEAR 1	22	7	33	24	14	100
YEAR 2	35	7	25	16	17	100
YEAR 3	24	9	29	18	20	100
YEAR 4	18	8	32	15	27	100
YEAR 5	15	10	41	18	16	100

YEAR	TOTAL NUMBER OF STAFF AT XYZ COMPANY BY YEAR
YEAR 1	3,500
YEAR 2	3,700
YEAR 3	4,500
YEAR 4	2,700
YEAR 5	3,200

Between which two years did the number of staff in HR change the most?

a. YEAR 1 – YEAR 2
b. YEAR 2 – YEAR 3
c. YEAR 3 – YEAR 4
d. YEAR 4 – YEAR 5
e. Cannot Say

SOLUTION TO QUESTION 9D

The first thing to do is to find out the HR staff numbers for each year. This is achieved by multiplying the percentage of HR staff by the total number of staff at XYZ Company for a particular year.

So, starting with YEAR 1:

HR staff as a percentage of total staff in YEAR 1 = 22%

As a decimal 22%$=\dfrac{22}{100}=$ **0.22**

Total number of Staff at XYZ Company in YEAR 1=3,500

Number of HR staff in YEAR 1=0.22×3,500

$$=770$$

YEAR 2

HR staff as a percentage of total staff in year 2=35%

As a decimal 35%$=\dfrac{35}{100}=$ **0.35**

Total number of Staff at XYZ Company in YEAR 2=3,700

Number of HR staff in YEAR 2=0.35×3,700

$$=1,295$$

YEAR 3

HR staff as a percentage of total staff in year 3=24%

As a decimal 24%$=\dfrac{24}{100}=$ **0.24**

Total number of Staff at XYZ Company in YEAR 3=4,500

Number of HR staff in YEAR 3=0.24×4,500

$$=1,081$$

YEAR 4

HR staff as a percentage of total staff in YEAR 4=18%

As a decimal 18%$=\dfrac{18}{100}=$ **0.18**

Total number of Staff at XYZ Company in YEAR 4=2,700

Number of HR staff in YEAR 4=0.18×2,700

$$=486$$

YEAR 5

HR staff as a percentage of total staff in YEAR 5=15%

As a decimal $15\% = \dfrac{15}{100} = 0.15$

Total number of Staff at XYZ Company in year 5=3,200

Number of HR staff in YEAR 5= 0.15×3,200

$$=480$$

Now that I have calculated the number of staff working in HR for each year, I can proceed to calculate which two years had the biggest change in HR staff. To find the biggest change in HR staff means finding the biggest difference in HR staff numbers between two consecutive years. The method is shown below:

YEAR 1 −YEAR 2

YEAR 1 HR staff numbers=770

YEAR 2 HR staff numbers=1,295

Change in HR staff numbers between YEAR 1 & YEAR 2=1,295−770

$$=525$$

YEAR 2 −YEAR 3

YEAR 2 HR staff numbers=1,295

YEAR 3 HR staff numbers= 1,080

Change in HR staff numbers between YEAR 2 & YEAR 3=1,295−1,080

$$=215$$

YEAR 3 −YEAR 4

YEAR 3 HR staff numbers=1,080

YEAR 4 HR staff numbers= 486

Change in HR staff numbers between YEAR 3 & YEAR 4=1,080−486

$$=594$$

YEAR 4 – YEAR 5

YEAR 4 HR staff numbers = 486

YEAR 5 HR staff numbers = 480

Change in HR staff numbers between YEAR 4 & YEAR 5 = 486 – 480

= 6

From the above calculations, YEAR 3 – YEAR 4 had the biggest change in the number of staff working within the HR function.

Summary table:

YEARS	CHANGE IN HR STAFF NUMBERS BETWEEN YEARS
YEAR 1 – YEAR 2	525
YEAR 2 – YEAR 3	215
YEAR 3 – YEAR 4	594
YEAR 4 – YEAR 5	6

The answer to question 9d is **c. YEAR 3 – YEAR 4**

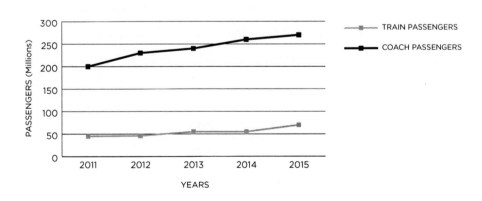

QUESTION 10
ANNUAL PERCENTAGE INCREASE & RATIOS

QUESTION 10A

Projected number of passengers (train and coach)

TRAIN PASSENGERS
COACH PASSENGERS

PASSENGERS (Millions)

300
250
200
150
100
50
0

2011   2012   2013   2014   2015

YEARS

It was once projected that from 2012 onwards, the number of train passengers would rise by 20% per annum. If this projection had proved to be correct, what would be the difference, approximately, between the projected numbers of train passengers shown on the graph above in 2015 and that according to the 20% per annum projection in 2015?

a. 16 million

b. 2 million

c. 22.5 million

d. 9.5 million

e. 16.5 million

SOLUTION TO QUESTION 10A

The question is asking for the difference between the projected data for train passengers shown on the graph for the year 2015 and data which once projected that from 2012 onwards, the number of train passengers would rise 20% per annum. Of course for this question, it is necessary to calculate the rise of 20% per annum in train passengers until 2015 only as this is what the question requires.

I start by noting the projected number of train passengers for the year 2015 from the projected number of passengers graph provided above.

Projected number of train passengers for the year 2015=**70 million (70,000,000)**

Next, I need to find what the projected number of train passengers are if an increase in train passengers of 20% per annum took place every year, starting in 2012 and ending in 2015. The method for doing this is explained below:

Projected number of train passengers for 2012=46 million (46,000,000).

The number of years between 2012 and 2015= **3 years**

I need to increase the projected number of train passengers for 2012 by 20% per annum until 2015, in other words, I need to increase 46 million by 20% for 3 years. To do this, I will firstly need to convert 20% into a decimal and add 1:

$$\text{As a decimal } 20\% = \frac{20}{100} = 0.20$$

I now add 1 to the decimal 0.20:

$$1 + 0.20 = 1.20$$

TIP: *The reason 1 is added to the decimal 0.20 is because the question asks for an increase every year by 20%. Multiplying any number by 1.20 would increase that number by 20%.*

To find the projected number of passengers for 2015 according to the increase of 20% per annum from 2012 until 2015 trend, I need to increase the projected number of passengers for 2012 by 20% every year for 3 years. This can be achieved by multiplying 46 million by 1.20 three times, which represents the 3 years:

Projected number of train passengers for 2015=46,000,000×**1.20×1.20×1.20**

Same as $(1.20)^3$

$$=46,000,000×(1.20)^3$$

$$=79,488,000 \text{ (79.488 million)}$$

Note that using the method 46,000,000×1.20×1.20×1.20 may have taken longer if the question had stated that the number of train passengers would increase by 20% per annum for 5 or more years rather than just 3, whereas using the method 46,000,000×$(1.20)^3$ would take the same amount of time regardless of how many years the increase took place over.

This is something you may want to take into consideration when deciding which method you want to use to answer similar questions.

Referring to the final part of the question:

"What would be the difference, approximately, between the projected numbers of train passengers shown on the graph above and that according to the 20% per annum projection in 2015?"

The difference is found by subtraction:

The projected numbers of train passengers shown on the graph in 2015= **70 million**

The passenger numbers according to the 20% per annum projection=**79.488 million**

Difference=79.488 million–70 million

=**9.488 million**

TIP: *When performing a calculation which requires the subtraction of two numbers that are both in millions, you can momentarily ignore the fact that* *the numbers are both in millions. So for example:*

$$Difference = 79.488 - 70$$

$$= 9.488$$

Then simply stick the word 'million' after 9.488

Now would be a good time to have a look at the answer options available. As 9.5 million is the closest to 9.488 million, the answer to question 10a is approximately **d. 9.5 million**

QUESTION 10B

Projected number of passengers (train and coach)

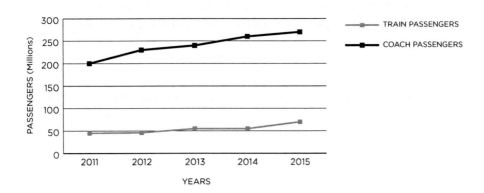

What is the projected ratio of Coach Passengers to Train passengers in 2012?"

a. 2:1

b. 3:1

c. 5:1

d. 2:3

e. Cannot say

SOLUTION TO QUESTION 10B

It is always best to understand what the question is actually asking for. In this particular case the question is actually asking:

"How many projected Coach Passengers are there per projected train passenger in 2012?"

The method of solving this question is to find both the projected number of train and coach passengers in 2012 from the graph and then calculate the ratio of coach passengers to train passengers as shown:

Projected number of train passengers in 2012= **46 million**

Projected number of coach passengers in 2012= **230 million**

Ratio of projected Coach passengers to projected Train passengers= **230÷46**

= **5**

TIP: *When it comes to ratios always make sure you divide by the quantity that comes after the word 'to'. So, in the above case, the ratio of projected coach passengers (230) TO projected train passengers (46) is required to be calculated. The projected train passengers comes after the word 'to' and so the projected coach passengers are divided by projected train passengers,*

$$230 \div 46 = 5$$

This means that there are 5 coach passengers for every train passenger, giving a ratio of 5:1

The answer to question 10b is **c. 5:1**

QUESTION 10C

Projected number of passengers (train and coach)

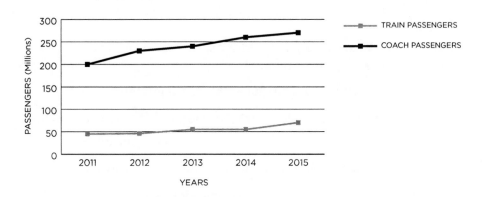

If every passenger is projected to spend £650 on train travel and £150 on coach travel annually each year, what will be the total projected amount spent over the period 2011-2015?

a. 822,450 million
b. 356,150 million
c. 150,000 million
d. 164,343 million
e. 455 million

SOLUTION TO QUESTION 10C

This question is very time consuming and it is vital that you work fast so that you can move on to other questions (unless a question like this comes up in the real exam as your final question!).

To calculate the total amount spent over the period 2011-2015 I need to multiply the total number of projected passengers for trains by the projected £650 annual spend and the total number of projected passengers for coaches by the projected £150 annual spend over this period.

Trains
Between and including the years 2011-2015, the total numbers of passengers are:

45 million+46 million+55 million+55 million+70 million=271 million

Projected spend for all projected train passengers=271 million×£ 650

=176,150 million

Coaches

Between and including the years 2011-2015, the total numbers of passengers added up are (in millions):

200+230+240+260+270=1,200 million

Projected spend for all projected coach passengers=1,200 million×£ 150

=180,000 million

Total projected amount to be spent=(176,150+180,000)million

=356,150 million

This means that total projected amount to be spent over the period 2011-2015 is **356,150 million.**

This is the final answer to question 10c

Note the importance of keeping the numbers with the word 'million' after their last digit rather than using the entire number to carry out calculations. It could get extremely confusing if you added six zeros to the end of an already large number such as 176,150 million for example, which would become 176,150,000,000.

QUESTION 11

DATA COMPARISON INVOLVING MULTIPLICATION, DIVISION, SUBTRACTION & ADDITION

QUESTION 11A

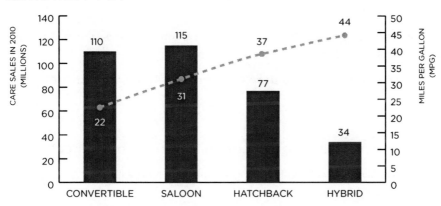

CARS SOLD IN 2010 (MILLIONS)

MILES PER GALLON (MPG)

CAR TYPE	CONVERTIBLE	SALOON	HATCHBACK	HYBRID
AVERAGE RETAIL PRICE	£26,000	£23,000	£18,000	£22,000
FUEL COST (PER UK GALLON)	£5.90	£5.30	£.5.10	£.3.95

One UK gallon is equivalent to 4.55 litres of fuel. Approximately how many litres of fuel would a journey of 350 miles consume using a hatchback?

a. 40 litres

b. 60 litres

c. 43 litres

d. 24 litres

e. Cannot Say

SOLUTION TO QUESTION 11A

All the information required is provided. I will need to make use of the miles per gallon of a hatchback and the conversion of gallon to litres. This immediately rules out the answer 'cannot say'.

From the graph, I can see that a hatchback's miles per UK gallon has a value of 37.

This means that for every 37 miles a hatchback travels, it has consumed one UK gallon. As the question states that one UK gallon is equivalent to 4.55 litres, it can be said that for every 37 miles a hatchback travels, it consumes 4.55 litres of fuel.

The next part of the question is asking how many litres a 350 mile journey would consume. This can be calculated as shown:

37 miles in a hatchback consumes 4.55 litres of fuel

350 miles in a hatchback consumes x litres of fuel

Cross multiplying gives the following equation, which will allow me to find the quantity x litres:

$$X \times 37 = 350 \times 4.55$$

$$X = \frac{350 \times 4.55}{37}$$

=43.04 litres (approximately)

A journey of 350 miles using a hatchback would consume approximately 43 litres of fuel.

The answer to question 11a) is **c. 43 litres**

QUESTION 11B

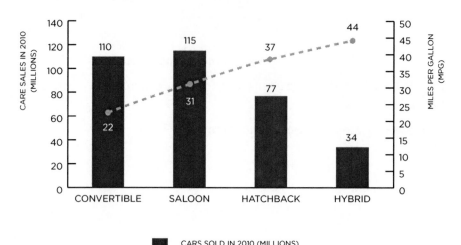

CARS SOLD IN 2010 (MILLIONS)

MILES PER GALLON (MPG)

CAR TYPE	CONVERTIBLE	SALOON	HATCHBACK	HYBRID
AVERAGE RETAIL PRICE	£19,500	£23,000	£18,000	£22,000
FUEL COST (PER UK GALLON)	£5.90	£5.30	£.5.10	£.3.95

A customer averages 15,000 miles per year. How many years would the customer need to drive the saloon car in order for it to be more economical than the convertible car, considering average retail prices and fuel costs for both car types?

a. 1 year
b. 2 years
c. 3 years
d. 4 years
e. 5 years

SOLUTION TO QUESTION 11B

A convertible has a much lower mile per UK gallon figure than a saloon car, which, in the long term will mean that it is more economical to drive a saloon car despite the higher average retail price of a saloon.

To find how long it takes a saloon to become more economical, use the following method. I will start with the costs per year for the convertible:

Convertible costs per year

A convertible achieves 22 miles per UK gallon i.e. Driving in a convertible for 22 miles consumes 1 UK gallon. After a year and 15,000 miles of driving, how many UK gallons will have been consumed by the convertible?

Well, if 22 miles consumes 1 UK gallon in a convertible,

15,000 miles consumes *x* UK gallons

Cross multiplying gives the following equation, which will allow me to find the quantity UK gallons:

$$X \times 22 = 15{,}000 \times 1$$

$$X = \frac{15{,}000 \times 1}{22}$$

$$= 681.82 \text{ UK gallons}$$

From the second table, the fuel cost per UK gallon is £5.90 for Convertible cars. So if the convertible consumes 681.82 UK gallons over the course of a year then the cost to run a convertible, driving an average of 15,000 miles per year is:

Cost per year of driving a convertible 15,000 miles= 681.82 × £ 5.90

=£ 4022.74

Note that the total cost incurred during the first year straight after purchasing the car will include the average retail price paid to purchase the car. So, for a convertible which has an average retail price of £19,500 the first year cost will be:

First year cost of driving a convertible 15,000 miles=£ 4022.74+£19,500

=£ 23,522.74

Saloon car costs

A saloon achieves 31 miles per UK gallon i.e. Driving in a saloon for 31 miles consumes 1 UK gallon. After a year and 15,000 miles of driving, how many UK gallons will have been consumed by the Saloon?

Well, if 31 miles consumes 1 UK gallon in a saloon,

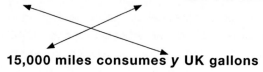

15,000 miles consumes *y* UK gallons

Cross multiplying gives the following equation, which will allow me to find the quantity   UK gallons:

$$y \times 31 = 15,000 \times 1$$

$$y = \frac{15,000 \times 1}{31}$$

=483.87 UK gallons

From the second table, the fuel cost per UK gallon is £ 5.90 for Saloon cars. So if the saloon consumes 483.87 UK gallons over the course of a year then the cost to run a saloon car, driving an average of 15,000 miles per year is:

Cost per year of driving a saloon 15,000 miles=**483.87×£ 5.90**

=£ 2854.83

Note that the total cost incurred during the first year straight after purchasing the car will include the average retail price paid to purchase the car. So, for a Saloon type car which has an average retail price of £ 23,000 the first year cost will be:

First year cost of driving a saloon 15,000 miles=**£ 2854.83+£ 23,000**

= £ 25,854.83

Now that both the Saloon and Convertible first year costs and costs per year have been calculated, it is possible to compare the costs of the two:

First year cost of driving a convertible 15,000 miles=£ 23,522.74

First year cost of driving a saloon 15,000 miles=£ 25,854.83

Difference in costs=£ 25,854.83–£ 23,522.74

=£ 2,332.09

It can now be seen that the first year cost of driving a convertible 15,000 miles is £ 2,332.09 cheaper than the first year cost of driving a saloon car the same distance. However, every year after the first year, the saloon car is cheaper to run than the convertible. The following shows and explains how the Saloon car becomes cheaper to run than the convertible:

Cost per year of driving a saloon 15,000 miles=483.87×£ 5.90

=£ 2854.83

Cost per year of driving a convertible 15,000 miles=681.82×£ 5.90

=£ 4022.74

Subtracting the costs per year of driving each car would tell me how much more the convertible costs to run per year than a saloon car:

Convertible cost per year –Saloon cost per year=£ 4022.74–£ 2854.83

=£ 1167.91

This means that it costs £ 1167.91 more to drive a convertible an average of 15,000 miles per year than a Saloon car. The following table shows how the initial saving of purchasing a convertible compared to a Saloon car slowly fades away (And in case you were wondering, no, I am not trying to sell you a car!)

Remember, the first year cost of driving a convertible 15,000 miles is £ 2,332.09 cheaper than the first year cost of driving a saloon car and a saloon car is £ 1167.91 cheaper to run per year thereafter. The following table summarises the savings:

SAVINGS* BY PURCHASING A CONVERTIBLE RATHER THAN A SALOON CAR	CONVERTIBLE	SALOON
1ST YEAR SAVING	£ 2,332.09	0
2ND YEAR SAVING	£ 2,332–£ 1167.91=£ 1164.09	0
3RD YEAR SAVING	£ 1164.09–£ 1167.91=–£ 3.82	+£ 3.82
4TH YEAR SAVING	–£ 3.82–£ 1167.91=–£ 1171.73	+£ 1171.73
5TH YEAR SAVING	–£ 1171.73–£ 1167.91=–£ 23396.64	+£ 2339.64

*BASED ON END OF YEAR COSTS, DRIVING AN AVERAGE OF 15,000 MILES

From this table, you can see that the Saloon car makes its first saving after the 3rd year of £ 3.82 or to put it another way, the convertible makes it first loss at the end of the 3rd year when compared to driving a saloon car the same distance. This means that the customer will have to drive the saloon for at least 3 years for it to be more economical than the convertible.

Thus, the answer to question 11b is **c. 3 years**

QUESTION 11C

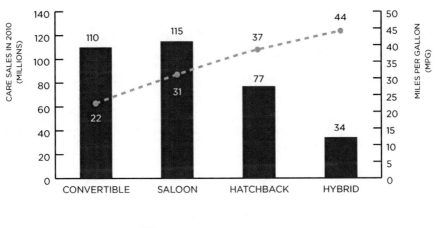

CARS SOLD IN 2010 (MILLIONS)

MILES PER GALLON (MPG)

CAR TYPE	CONVERTIBLE	SALOON	HATCHBACK	HYBRID
AVERAGE RETAIL PRICE	£26,000	£23,000	£18,000	£22,000
FUEL COST (PER UK GALLON)	£5.90	£5.30	£.5.10	£.3.95

Which type of car generated the largest amount of money in terms of sales for the year 2010?

a. Convertible

b. Saloon

c. Hatchback

d. Hybrid

SOLUTION TO QUESTION 11C

This is a tricky question. You may have instantly assumed that because 'saloon' has the highest amount of sales for 2010 that this is the answer.

Because the question asks for the 'largest amount of money generated in terms of sales' and the graph only contains the number of people who purchased and not the amount spent one cannot simply read off the graph for the highest number of sales and assume that the type of car with the highest number of people who purchased in 2010 means the highest amount of money generated.

The correct method for arriving at the answer is given below:

Convertible

Amount of money generated per sale of convertible type cars (average retail price) is given in the table as £ 26,000

From the graph, there were 110 million customers who purchased a convertible in 2010.

*Therefore, the money generated by selling convertibles to 110 million customers =£26,000×110 million=£ **286,000 million***

TIP: *When dealing with a question such as this, where a comparison needs to be made between data to find the largest or lowest quantity, save time by leaving the prefix 'million' as it is. Note that the word 'million' appears before and after the equals sign i.e. it hasn't been involved in the calculation.*

But remember the key to getting the correct answer quickly is consistency. Since I have used the format £26,000×110 million=2860000 million here, I must use this format for all other calculations in this question.

Saloon

Amount of money generated per sale of saloon type cars (average retail price) is given in the table as £23,000

From the graph, there were 115 million customers who purchased a saloon in 2010.

*Therefore, the money generated by selling saloons to 115 million customers =£23,000×115 million=£ **264,5000 million***

Note that to avoid confusion; I have used the same format here as I did for the convertible calculation.

Hatchback

Amount of money generated per sale of hatchback type cars (average retail price) is given in the table as £ 18,000

From the graph, there were 77 million customers who purchased a hatchback in 2010.

Therefore, the money generated by selling hatchbacks to 77 million customers =£ 18,000×77 million=£ 138,6000 million

Hybrid

Amount of money generated per sale of hybrid type cars (average retail price) is given in the table as £ 22,000

From the graph, there were 34 million customers who purchased a hybrid in 2010.

Therefore, the money generated by selling hybrids to 34 million customers =£ 22,000×34 million=£ 74,8000 million

Summary table

CAR TYPE	CONVERTIBLE	SALOON	HATCHBACK	HYBRID
MONEY GENERATED (MILLIONS)	£ 286,0000	£ 264,5000	£ 138,6000	£ 748,000

It is clear that the sales of convertible cars generated the highest amount of money and the answer to question 11c is **a. Convertible**.

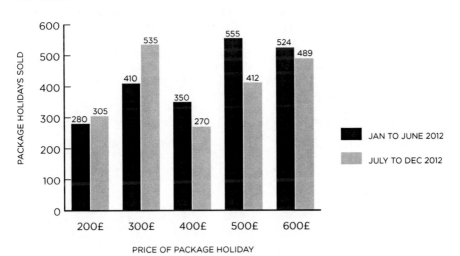

QUESTION 12
DATA INTERPRETATION/ ANALYSIS OF HOLIDAY SALES

QUESTION 12A

PACKAGE HOLIDAYS SOLD

	200£	300£	400£	500£	600£
JAN TO JUNE 2012	280	410	350	555	524
JULY TO DEC 2012	305	535	270	412	489

PRICE OF PACKAGE HOLIDAY

■ JAN TO JUNE 2012

▨ JULY TO DEC 2012

The total amount of £300 package holidays sold in 2012 represents 60% of the sales target required to be reached annually by each travel agent office. What would be the total target for 7 travel agent offices in the year 2012?

a. 312,000

b. 11,025

c. 21,295

d. 456

SOLUTION TO QUESTION 12A

The total amount of £300 package holidays sold = 410 + 535 = 945

945 is equivalent to 60% of the annual sales target. In order to solve this question, 100% of the annual sales target needs to be known. This can be achieved by the following calculation:

$$100\% \text{ of annual sales target} = \frac{945}{60\%} = \frac{945}{0.6} = 1575$$

Therefore, 1575 holidays need to be sold to reach the annual target for each travel agent office.

If one travel agent office has a target of selling 1575 holidays annually then 7 travel agent offices would have 7 times this amount.

Total sales target for 7 travel agent offices in the year 2012=1575 x 7=11,025

In order for 7 travel agent offices to meet their target in the year 2012 11,025 holidays need to be sold.

The answer is b. 11,025.

QUESTION 12B

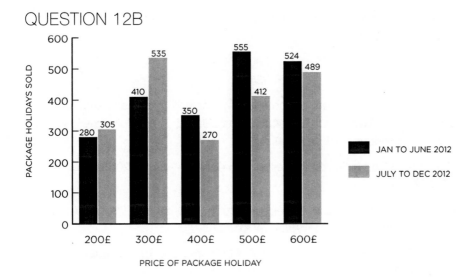

The commission paid to each sales agent who sells a holiday is 2.5% of the amount the holiday was sold for. How much commission is paid out in total to all sales agents for the year 2012?

a. £ 43,495
b. £ 50,250
c. £ 33,333
d. £ 25,000
e. None of the above

SOLUTION TO QUESTION 12B

Calculating the commission received by sales agents for holidays worth £200

If a holiday sells for £200, the agent get's 2.5% commission. To work out how much commission the sales agent gets for selling a £200 holiday multiply £200 by 2.5%.

It would be easier to convert 2.5% into a decimal before multiplying it with £200. To convert 2.5% into a decimal divide it by 100.

$$2.5\% \div 100 = 0.025$$

Therefore the commission received by a sales agent selling a £200 holiday would be:

$$£200 \times 0.025 = £5$$

However, from the graph it can be seen that for the year 2012 the number of £200 holidays sold

$$= 280 + 305$$
$$= 585$$

Therefore the total amount of commission received by sales agents for selling 585 holidays worth £200 can be calculated by multiplying £5 with the amount of holidays sold for £200.

Total commission received for selling 585 holidays worth £200 each = £5 x 585 = £2925

This process now needs to be repeated for holidays worth £300, £400 and £500 using the same commission rate of 2.5%.

Calculating the commission received by sales agents for holidays worth £300

The commission received by a sales agent selling a £300 holiday would be:

$$£300 \times 0.025 = £7.50$$

From the graph it can be seen that for the year 2012 the number of £300 holidays sold

$$= 410 + 535$$
$$= 945$$

Total commission received for selling 945 holidays worth £300 each = £7.50 x 945 = £7087.50

Calculating the commission received by sales agents for holidays worth £400

The commission received by a sales agent selling a £400 holiday would be:

$$£400 \times 0.025 = 10$$

From the graph it can be seen that for the year 2012 the number of £400 holidays sold

$$= 350 + 270$$
$$= 620$$

Total commission received for selling 620 holidays worth £400 each = £10 x 620 = £6200

Calculating the commission received by sales agents for holidays worth £500

The commission received by a sales agent selling a £500 holiday would be:

$$£500 \times 0.025 = £12.50$$

From the graph it can be seen that for the year 2012 the number of £500 holidays sold

$$= 555 + 412$$
$$= 967$$

Total commission received for selling 967 holidays worth £500 each = £12.50 x 967 = £12,087.50

Calculating the commission received by sales agents for holidays worth £600

The commission received by a sales agent selling a £600 holiday would be:

$$£600 \times 0.025 = £15$$

From the graph it can be seen that for the year 2012 the number of £600 holidays sold

$$= 524 + 489$$
$$= 1013$$

Total commission received for selling 1013 holidays worth £600 each = £15 x 1013 = £15,195

To calculate the total amount of commission paid to all sales agents for the year 2012 simply add up all the commissions received i.e. add the commissions received from total sales of holidays worth £200,£300,£400, £500 and £600.

Total commission paid to all sales agents

$$= £2,925 + £7,087.50 + £6,200 + £12,087.50 + £15,195 = \textbf{£43,495}$$

The answer is a. **£43,495** in total was paid out to sales agents in 2012 as their commission.

QUESTION 12C

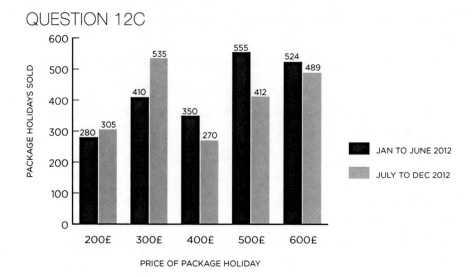

What is the total value of all holidays sold in the year 2012?

a. £6000
b. £3995
c. £45,000
d. £1,254,658
e. £1,739,800

SOLUTION TO QUESTION 12C

The table below summarises the total amount of holidays sold.

PRICE OF HOLIDAY	HOLIDAYS SOLD BETWEEN JAN TO JUNE 2012	HOLIDAYS SOLD BETWEEN JULY TO DEC 2012	TOTAL HOLIDAYS SOLD IN 2012
£200	280	305	585
£300	410	535	945
£400	350	270	620
£500	555	412	967
£600	524	489	1013

From the table it can be seen that 585 holidays worth £200 were sold in 2012. Multiplying 585 by £200 will give the total value of all £200 holidays sold in 2012.

Total value of all £200 holidays sold in 2012= 585 x £200
= £117,000

Now repeat the process for £300, £400, £500 and £600 holidays.

Total value of all £300 holidays sold in 2012= 945 x £300
= £283,500

Total value of all £400 holidays sold in 2012= 620 x £400
= £248,000

Total value of all £500 holidays sold in 2012= 967 x £500
= £483,500

Total value of all £600 holidays sold in 2012= 1013 x £600
= £607,800

The total value of all holidays sold in the year 2012 can now be found by adding up all of the above.

Total value of all holidays sold in the year 2012

= £117,000 + £283,500 + £248,000 + £483,500 + £607,800

= **£1,739,800**

The answer is e. £1,739,800

QUESTION 12D

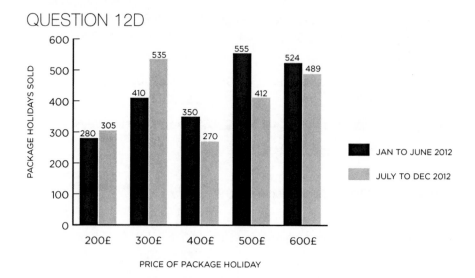

PRICE OF PACKAGE HOLIDAY

In 2013 it is expected that the difference in package holiday sales between 2012's July - Dec and January-June period is going to increase by an eighth. What is the projected difference in package holiday sales between Jan- June and July-December for 2013 in pounds?

a. £ 23,995

b. £ 45,695

c. £ 20,875

d. £ 16,347

SOLUTION TO QUESTION 12D

Firstly calculate the difference for 2012 sales as shown:

	JAN TO JUNE 2012	JULY TO DEC 2012	DIFFERENCE (PACKAGE HOLIDAYS SOLD)	DIFFERENCE (£)
£200	280	305	25	£ 5000
£300	535	410	125	£ 37,500
£400	350	270	80	£ 32,000
£500	555	412	143	£ 71,500
£600	524	489	35	£ 21,000
			408	**£ 167,000**

Now increase the total price difference of £167,000 by an eighth. How to do this is shown below.

$$\text{An eighth} = \frac{1}{8} = 0.125$$

To increase a number by an eighth add 1 to the decimal form of an eighth and multiply by the number you want to increase by an eighth.

$$0.125 + 1 = 1.125$$

It is now possible to increase £167,000 by an eighth simply by multiplying it with 1.125

$$£167,000 \times 1.125 = £20,275$$

Therefore, the projected difference in package holiday sales between July-Dec and Jan- June for 2013 is c. **£ 20,875**

QUESTION 12E

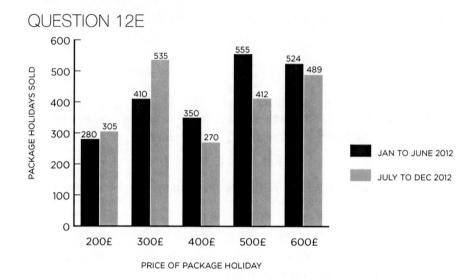

PRICE OF PACKAGE HOLIDAY

If £300 package holidays were put on special offer of 25% off the normal price during the months Jan-June 2012 how much money would have been lost due to this special offer compared to if the price had remained at £300?

a. £ 1,200
b. £ 30,750
c. £ 26,596
d. £ 12,559
e. £ 33,597

SOLUTION TO QUESTION 12E

$$25\% = 0.25$$
$$25\% \text{ of } £300 = 0.25 \times £300 = £75$$

This means that customers would be given £75 off the price of a £300 package holiday. They would therefore pay £300 - £75 = £225 each for their holidays (normally £300).

From the graph, 410 holidays in the period between Jan-June 2012 were sold normally worth £300. In total this would make: 410 x £300 = £123,000

However, the holidays were sold for £225 after a 25% discount was applied. In total, this makes:

410 x £225 = £92,250

To find the amount of money lost due to the special offer subtract the two:

£123,000 - £92,250 = **£30,750**

Therefore, the answer is b. **£30,750** is lost due to this special offer.

QUESTION 12F

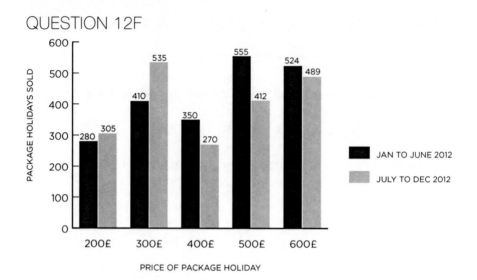

If the price of a £300 package holiday was reduced by 25% between Jan-June 2012 but the same amount of holidays were sold as the July-Dec 2012 period, how much extra money would have been generated from these sales?

a. £ 20,555
b. £ 22,433
c. £ 15,495
d. £ 28,125
e. £ 66,546

SOLUTION TO QUESTION 12F

$$25\% = 0.25$$
$$25\% \text{ of } £300 = 0.25 \times £300 = £75$$

This means that customers would be given £75 off the price of a £300 package holiday. They would therefore pay £300 - £75 = £225 each for their holidays (normally £300).

If the sales increased from 410 package holidays sold to the July-Dec 2012 level of 535 sold this would mean that an extra 535-410 = 125 holidays were sold in the Jan-June 2012 period.

If every holiday sold that was normally £300 is now selling for £225 the extra money generated from these sales can be found by multiplying 125 by £225.

$$125 \times £225 = £28,125$$

The answer is d. **£ 28,125**

QUESTION 13
PERCENTAGES & DATA ANALYSIS

QUESTION 13A

Number of deliveries (June 2012)

DELIVERY AREA	TRUCK A	TRUCK B	TRUCK C	TRUCK D	TRUCK E
Southampton	409	211	433	256	890
Portsmouth	333	412	650	777	312
Cardiff	324	435	456	786	675
Brighton	543	756	357	890	879
Edinburgh	676	234	123	675	355

What was the total number of days spent on deliveries to Cardiff in June if 350 deliveries can be achieved per day?

a. 5 days
b. 6 days
c. 7 days
d. 8 days
e. 9 days

SOLUTION TO QUESTION 13A

Total deliveries to Cardiff in the month of June = 324 + 435 + 456 + 786 + 675

= 2676

If 350 deliveries can be achieved per day the amount of days spent on deliveries to Cardiff =

$$\frac{2676}{350} = 7.65 \text{ days}$$

Since there is no such thing as 0.65 of a day, the answer to this question is d. 8 days.

QUESTION 13B

Number of deliveries (June 2012)

DELIVERY AREA	TRUCK A	TRUCK B	TRUCK C	TRUCK D	TRUCK E
Southampton	409	211	433	256	890
Portsmouth	333	412	650	777	312
Cardiff	324	435	456	786	675
Brighton	543	756	357	890	879
Edinburgh	676	234	123	675	355

There were 2 drivers in the month of June for Truck B. Driver 1 delivered 25% more than driver 2 in June. If the drivers are paid £52.50 per delivery calculate the amount of money driver 1 made

a. £ 1,500
b. £25,556. 60
c. £7987.20
d. £6995.40
e. None of the above

SOLUTION TO QUESTION 13B

Total amount of deliveries by truck B in June = 211 + 412 + 435 + 756 + 234

$$= 2048$$

AMOUNT OF DELIVERIES CARRIED OUT BY EACH DRIVER

If both drivers had delivered the same amount, this would have been 50% of the total deliveries each. However, driver 1 delivered 25% more than driver 2. Therefore, in total, driver 1 made 50%+25%=75% of the deliveries which means that driver 2 only made 25% of the deliveries.

To calculate exactly how many deliveries were made by driver 1, multiply the percentage delivered by the total amount of deliveries by truck B.

Driver 1:

2048 x 75% = 2048 x 0.75 = 1536 deliveries

For comparison, since there were 2048 deliveries in total, it follows that driver 2 must have delivered the remaining goods which were 2048 - 1536 = 512 deliveries.

The question states that drivers are paid £52.50 per delivery. Because driver 1 carried out 1536 deliveries the total amount paid to driver 1 can be calculated by multiplying the amount of deliveries with the amount paid to drivers per delivery.

$$1536 \times £5.25 = \textbf{£7987.20}$$

Driver 1 gets paid £7987.20 for 1536 deliveries in the month of June.

QUESTION 13C

Number of deliveries (June 2012)

DELIVERY AREA	TRUCK A	TRUCK B	TRUCK C	TRUCK D	TRUCK E
Southampton	409	211	433	256	890
Portsmouth	333	412	650	777	312
Cardiff	324	435	456	786	675
Brighton	543	756	357	890	879
Edinburgh	676	234	123	675	355

Put the trucks in increasing order of total number of deliveries in June (starting with the lowest number of deliveries).

a. C,B,A,E,D
b. A,B,C,D,E
c. B,C,A,D,E
d. C,B,D,A,E
e. D,A,B,C,E

SOLUTION TO QUESTION 13C

Total deliveries in June

Truck A: 2285

Truck B: 2048

Truck C: 2019

Truck D: 3384

Truck E: 3111

Therefore from lowest to highest the answer is a. : **C, B, A, E, D**

QUESTION 13D

Number of deliveries (June 2012)

DELIVERY AREA	TRUCK A	TRUCK B	TRUCK C	TRUCK D	TRUCK E
Southampton	409	211	433	256	890
Portsmouth	333	412	650	777	312
Cardiff	324	435	456	786	675
Brighton	543	756	357	890	879
Edinburgh	676	234	123	675	355

It is expected that there will be a 30% increase in demand for deliveries in June 2013 and a new truck will need to join the fleet to cope with the demand. If the new truck covers all the new deliveries then how many deliveries in total with the new truck have to deliver next June?

a. 1,650
b. 2,300
c. 3,854
d. 4,100
e. 5,430

SOLUTION TO QUESTION 13D

Total amount of deliveries for June 2012 = 2285 + 2048 + 2019 + 3384 + 3111
= 12,847

The question states it is expected that the total amount of deliveries for June 2012 increases by 30% to make the total amount of June 2013 deliveries. To increase 12847 by 30% first write 30% as a decimal:

$$30\% = 0.3$$

Because an increase is required add 1 to this and then multiply with 12847:

$$0.3 + 1 = 1.3$$

$$1.3 \times 12,847 = 16,701$$

This means that there will be an estimated 16701 deliveries in total for June 2013.

The new truck entering service in 2013 will have to carry out the following amount of deliveries:

16701 - 12847 = **3854 deliveries**

The answer to this question is c. **3854 deliveries**.

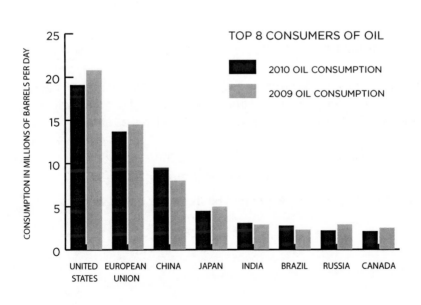

QUESTION 14
PERCENTAGE INCREASE & DECREASE/ DATA INTERPRETATION & ANALYSIS/ CONVERSION OF UNITS

QUESTION 14A

TOP 8 CONSUMERS OF OIL

CONSUMPTION IN MILLIONS OF BARRELS PER DAY

■ 2010 OIL CONSUMPTION

▨ 2009 OIL CONSUMPTION

UNITED STATES · EUROPEAN UNION · CHINA · JAPAN · INDIA · BRAZIL · RUSSIA · CANADA

If one barrel equals 158.99 litres how many litres of oil were consumed per day in 2010 in total by the 8 countries?

a. 10,540 million litres

b. 9,990 million litres

c. 6,500 million litres

d. 2,500 million litres

e. 9,603 million litres

SOLUTION TO QUESTION 14A

Oil Consumption in 2010 by all countries can be found by adding up the consumption for all countries in 2010 (remember that oil consumption is in millions) :

OIL CONSUMER	OIL CONSUMPTION IN BARRELS PER DAY FOR 2010
United States	19.2 million
European Union	13.8 million
China	9.5 million
Japan	4.5 million
India	3.2 million
Brazil	3.8 million
Russia	3.2 million
Canada	3.2 million
TOTAL CONSUMPTION IN 2010	**= 60.4 MILLION barrels per day**

If 60.4 million barrels per day were consumed in 2010 and one barrel equals 158.99 litres then to find how many litres were consumed per day multiply the number of barrels consumed per day by 158.99 litres as shown:

Litres of oil consumed per day = 60.4 million x 158.99

= **9603 million litres**

The answer is e. that in total, **9,603 million litres** per day were consumed in 2010.

QUESTION 14B

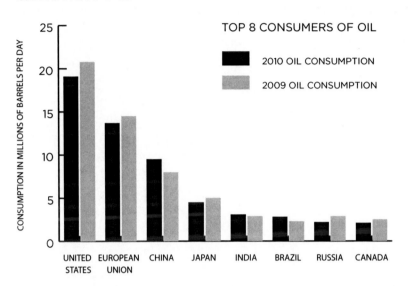

TOP 8 CONSUMERS OF OIL

- 2010 OIL CONSUMPTION
- 2009 OIL CONSUMPTION

If there are 365 days per year, in total, how much oil was consumed in the year 2010?

(I barrel= 158.99 litres)

a. 3,505,095 million litres
b. 4,505,095 million litres
c. 5,715,583 million litres
d. 2,132,125 million litres
e. 1,243,147 million litres

SOLUTION TO QUESTION 14B

In the previous question it was worked out that in total 9603 million litres per day were consumed in 2010. If this is consumption per day and there are 365 days in a year, then by multiplying 9603 million litres by 365 it is possible to calculate the total consumption for the year 2010.

Total amount of litres consumed in 2010 = 9603 million x 365
= **3,505,095 million**

The answer is a. in total, **3,505,095 million litres** of oil were consumed by the top 8 oil consuming regions of the world in 2010. That sure is a lot of oil for a year!

QUESTION 14C

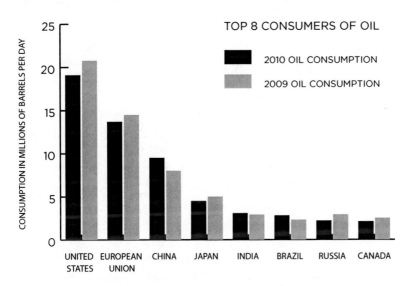

Which region showed the greatest percentage increase in the consumption of oil per day between 2009 and 2010?

a. United States
b. India
c. Brazil
d. China
e. Canada

SOLUTION TO QUESTION 14C

COUNTRY	2009 CONSUMPTION PER DAY	2010 CONSUMPTION PER DAY
Brazil	2.3 million	2.5 million
India	2.8 million	3.1 million
China	7.9 million	9.5 million

COUNTRY	INCREASE (HIGHEST - LOWEST)	PERCENTAGE INCREASE (HIGHEST - LOWEST) / LOWEST
Brazil	(2.5 - 2.3) million = 0.2 million	$\dfrac{0.2}{2.3} \times 100\% = 8.7\%$
India	(3.1 - 2.8) million = 0.3 million	$\dfrac{0.3}{2.8} \times 100\% = 10.7\%$
China	(9.5 - 7.9) million = 1.6 million	$\dfrac{1.6}{7.9} \times 100\% = 20.3\%$

It can now be clearly seen that China has the greatest percentage increase in the consumption of oil per day between 2009 and 2010 with a percentage increase of 20.3%

The answer is therefore **d. China.**

QUESTION 14D

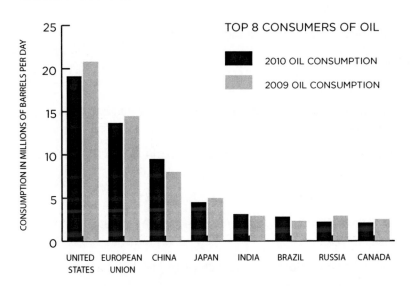

Assuming that the United States percentage decrease in oil consumption per day from 2009 to 2010 remained constant until 2018 what will be the estimated oil consumption per day for the United States in 2018?"

a. 1.26 million
b. 1.3 million
c. 0.5 million
d. 998,565
e. 1.25 million

SOLUTION TO QUESTION 14C

$$\text{Percentage decrease} = \frac{\text{Highest - Lowest}}{\text{Highest}}$$

Therefore, the percentage decrease for United States oil consumption per day from 2009 to 2010

$$\frac{(27 - 19.2) \text{ million}}{27 \text{ million}} \times 100\%$$

$$= 28.9\%$$

This means that the consumption per day decreases every year in the united states by 28.9% until 2013.

Now, subtract 100% from the percentage decrease of 28.9%:

100% - 28.9% = 71.1%

As a decimal 71.1% = 0.711

0.711 is known as a multiplier. If it is multiplied with any number it will decrease that number by 28.9%.

In order to find what the oil consumption will be in the United States for the year 2018 (which is 8 years ahead of 2010) the calculation is:

$$2010 \text{ oil consumption per day} \times (0.711)^8$$

The power of 8 next to the 0.711 in the above equation indicates that there are 8 decreases (8 years).

United States expected oil consumption per day in 2018

$$= 19.2 \text{ million} \times (0.711)^8$$

$$= \textbf{1.25 million}$$

The answer is e.**1.25 million**

QUESTION 14E

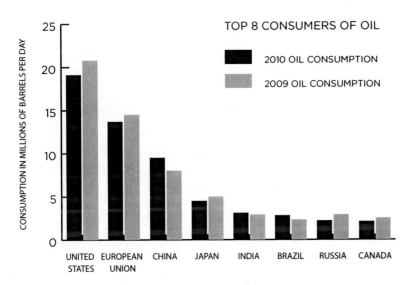

In Brazil, if the oil consumption per day continued to rise by 8.7% until 2014 and then decreased by 6% from 2014 to 2016 what would be the oil consumption per day in 2016?

a. 4.6 million
b. 1.25 million
c. 3.08 million
d. 0.9 million
e. None of the above

SOLUTION TO QUESTION 14E

8.7% as a decimal= 0.087

To increase any number by 8.7% add 1 to its decimal version:

$$0.087 + 1 = 1.087$$

Oil Consumption per day in Brazil in 2014 = 2.5 million x $(1.087)^4$

$$= 3.49 \text{ million}$$

The questions states that it then decreases by 6% from 2014 to 2016.

To find the multiplier which will reduce any number it is multiplied with by 6% first subtract 6% from 100% as shown:

$$100\% - 6\% = 94\%$$

Now convert 94% into a decimal:

94% as a decimal= 0.94

0.94 is known as the multiplier which will decrease any number it is multiplied with by 6%.

In 2014 it has been calculated that the oil consumption per day in Brazil will be 3.49 million. The oil consumption per day decreases by 6% until 2016 which is a 2 year period. The equation is therefore:

2016 oil consumption per day in Brazil = 3.49 million x $(0.94)^2$

$$= \textbf{3.08 million}$$

The answer is c. **3.08 million**

MOCK EXAM
QUESTIONS

Instructions:

- You have 25 minutes to answer 18 questions.

- You are strongly advised to time yourself (note that in the actual online exam, a timer will be provided for you on the same screen that the question and multiple choice answers appear).

- Aim to spend no longer than 1 minute 20 seconds on each of the following 18 questions.

- Work quickly and accurately and if you get stuck on a question move on to the next (unless it is your final question).

- Some online numerical reasoning tests do not allow you to return and check your previous answers, so it is best to practice getting used to not having to return to questions once you have moved on to the next.

- Finally, good luck!

QUESTION 1

2010 DRINK SALES IN SUPERMARKETS BY UK REGION (100,000s)

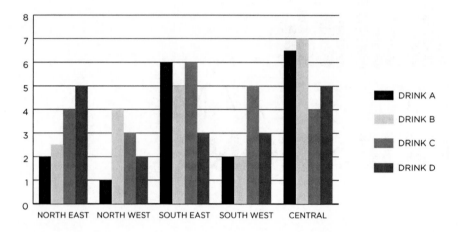

Total sales for all UK regions combined are a fifth of the sales of drink in supermarkets for the entire USA. If the south west region of the USA accounts for 30% of total USA drink sales in supermarkets, how many drinks were sold in south west USA in 2010?

a. 33,400,000
b. 11,700,000
c. 14,500,324
d. 6,995,000
e. 21,655,765

QUESTION 2

2010 DRINK SALES IN SUPERMARKETS BY UK REGION (100,000s)

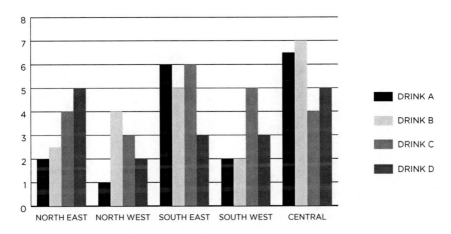

What percentage of total drinks sales from all regions combined did the South East and Central region approximately contain?

a. 62.4%

b. 54.5%

c. 33.3%

d. 22.5%

e. 20%

QUESTION 3

2010 DRINK SALES IN SUPERMARKETS BY UK REGION (100,000s)

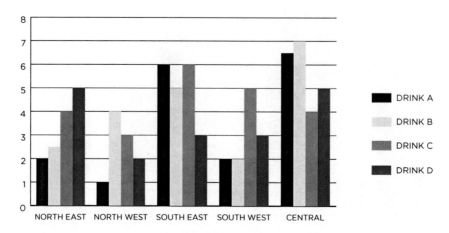

What was the total percentage increase for Drink's A and C combined when comparing North East and South East regional supermarket sales?

a. 130%
b. 75%
c. 15%
d. 220%
e. 250%

QUESTION 4

Number of machines that need upgrading and location

LOCATION	NUMBER OF MACHINES THAT NEED UPGRADING	COST PER MACHINE REPLACED (£)
MIKES FACTORY	6,500	120
STEINER MANUFACTURING	3,300	95
CAPITAL MOTORS	860	310
MACHINERY FACTORY INC.	40	205

The first 500 machines that need upgrading will be replaced by 5 machines for every machine that needs to be upgraded.

The next 500 machines that need upgrading will be replaced by 3 machines for every machine that needs upgrading.

Any machines that need upgrading thereafter will be replaced by 2 machines for every machine that needs to be upgraded.

How many machines were replaced at Mikes Factory?

a. 6,500
b. 11,000
c. 14,595
d. 15,000
e. 4,325

QUESTION 5

Number of machines that need upgrading and location

LOCATION	NUMBER OF MACHINES THAT NEED UPGRADING	COST PER MACHINE REPLACED (£)
MIKES FACTORY	6,500	120
STEINER MANUFACTURING	3,300	95
CAPITAL MOTORS	860	310
MACHINERY FACTORY INC.	40	205

The first 500 machines that need upgrading will be replaced by 5 machines for every machine that needs to be upgraded.

The next 500 machines that need upgrading will be replaced by 3 machines for every machine that needs upgrading.

Any machines that need upgrading thereafter will be replaced by 2 machines for every machine that needs to be upgraded.

How much would it cost to replace all the machines that need upgrading at Steiner manufacturing?

a. £ 125,000
b. £ 16,000
c. £ 817,000
d. £ 33,995
e. £ 275,430

QUESTION 6

Number of machines that need upgrading and location

LOCATION	NUMBER OF MACHINES THAT NEED UPGRADING	COST PER MACHINE REPLACED (£)
MIKES FACTORY	6,500	120
STEINER MANUFACTURING	3,300	95
CAPITAL MOTORS	860	310
MACHINERY FACTORY INC.	40	205

The first 500 machines that need upgrading will be replaced by 5 machines for every machine that needs to be upgraded.

The next 500 machines that need upgrading will be replaced by 3 machines for every machine that needs upgrading.

Any machines that need upgrading thereafter will be replaced by 2 machines for every machine that needs to be upgraded.

What is the total cost of replacing machines at all locations combined?

a. £ 3,000,420
b. £ 3,676,800
c. £ 2,130,020
d. £ 335,995,000
e. £ 3,767,800

QUESTION 7

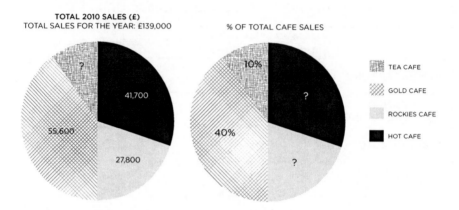

TOTAL 2010 SALES (£)
TOTAL SALES FOR THE YEAR: £139,000

% OF TOTAL CAFE SALES

TEA CAFE
GOLD CAFE
ROCKIES CAFE
HOT CAFE

What was the percentage of total sales for 'Rockies cafe' according to the 2010 sales figures?

a. 15%
b. 12%
c. 23%
d. 45%
e. 20%

QUESTION 8

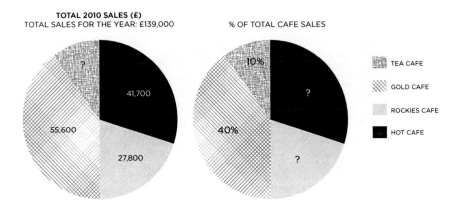

TOTAL 2010 SALES (£)
TOTAL SALES FOR THE YEAR: £139,000

% OF TOTAL CAFE SALES

TEA CAFE
GOLD CAFE
ROCKIES CAFE
HOT CAFE

What was the percentage of total sales for 'hot cafe'?

a. 17%
b. 25%
c. 18%
d. 30%
e. 16%

QUESTION 9

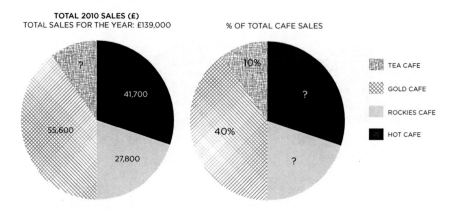

TOTAL 2010 SALES (£)
TOTAL SALES FOR THE YEAR: £139,000

% OF TOTAL CAFE SALES

TEA CAFE
GOLD CAFE
ROCKIES CAFE
HOT CAFE

What was the 2010 sales figure for the 'tea cafe'?

a. 13,900

b. 12,500

c. 16,200

d. 14,250

e. Cannot Say

QUESTION 10

Today's exchange rates for dollars
(rates are stated as dollars per the currency listed)

	CLOSING POINT	TODAY'S HIGH	TODAY'S LOW	CLOSING POINT CHANGE FROM YESTERDAY
STERLING	35.21	36.31	33.18	+0.42
EURO	20.19	22.04	18.70	-0.32
YEN	0.25	0.28	0.23	+0.10

If the Today's high/ Closing point ratio for Yen is constant, what would 'Yesterday's high' for the Yen have been approximately?

a. 0.17
b. 0.21
c. 0.24
d. 0.28
e. 0.14

QUESTION 11

Today's exchange rates for dollars
(rates are stated as dollars per the currency listed)

	CLOSING POINT	TODAY'S HIGH	TODAY'S LOW	CLOSING POINT CHANGE FROM YESTERDAY
STERLING	35.21	36.31	33.18	+0.42
EURO	20.19	22.04	18.70	-0.32
YEN	0.25	0.28	0.23	+0.10

A debt of £1,000,000 is owed and $45,000,000 was exchanged into Sterling at Today's high. Approximately how many pounds sterling would be leftover or still owing, if any, after paying the debt?

a. £ 239,328 still owing
b. £ 133,299 still owing
c. £ 39,023,333 left over
d. £ 239,328 left over
e. £ 150,763 left over

QUESTION 12

Today's exchange rates for dollars
(rates are stated as dollars per the currency listed)

	CLOSING POINT	TODAY'S HIGH	TODAY'S LOW	CLOSING POINT CHANGE FROM YESTERDAY
STERLING	35.21	36.31	33.18	+0.42
EURO	20.19	22.04	18.70	-0.32
YEN	0.25	0.28	0.23	+0.10

How many Euros would you get for £ 300 sterling yesterday, according to the closing point exchange rate (rounded to the nearest 10)?

a. 500 EUROS
b. 520 EUROS
c. 480 EUROS
d. 460 EUROS
e. 510 EUROS

QUESTION 13

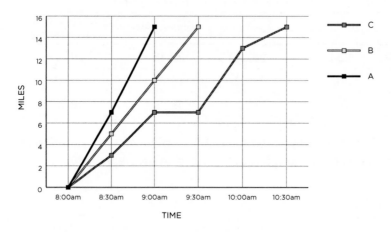

TIME TAKEN TO TRAVEL HOME FROM WORK

100 miles = 161 km

If Danny's train leaves at 8.30am rather than 8am and maintained an average speed of 48.3 km/h throughout the journey to work without any delays, what time would Danny arrive at work?

a. 9.45 am
b. 8.30 am
c. 9.15am
d. 9.00am
e. 10am

QUESTION 14

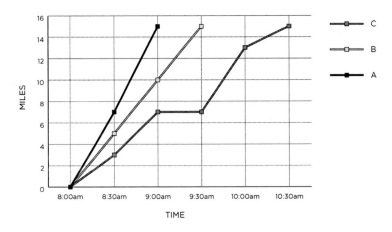

TIME TAKEN TO TRAVEL HOME FROM WORK

100 miles = 161 km

At 112.63 km from Sam's house, the bus encountered mechanical fail-ure and Sam had to wait from 9am to 9.30am for a replacement bus to arrive so that he could complete his journey to work. If the bus had not broken down and kept the same average speed as it did from 8am to 9am, approximately what time would Sam have arrived at work?

a. 10.15 am
b. 9.30 am
c. 10.39 am
d. 10.09 am
e. 9.55 am

QUESTION 15

TIME TAKEN TO TRAVEL HOME FROM WORK

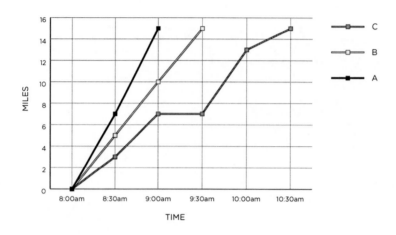

100 miles = 161 km

At 8.30am, Anita receives a call from her boss telling her to be at work for 9am. What is the minimum speed Anita would need to drive at, in km/h from 8.30am onwards in order to be at work for 9am?

a. 43.5 km/h

b. 32.2 km/h

c. 29.8 km/h

d. 44.3 km/h

e. 31.3 km/h

QUESTION 16

Workforce UK's revenue and operating profit

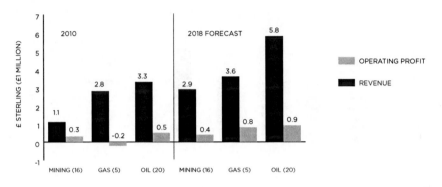

NUMBER AND TYPE OF COMPANIES OPERATING WITHIN "WORKFORCE UK"

What is the forecasted percentage increase in Revenue for the Gas industry between 2010 and 2018?

a. 28.6%

b. 82.4%

c. 63.2%

d. 131.2%

e. 54.3%

QUESTION 17

Workforce UK's revenue and operating profit

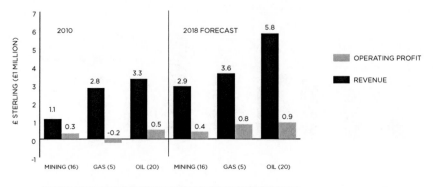

What will be the annual percentage increase in the Oil industries revenue, taking into account the total increase between the 2010 oil revenue and 2018 forecasted oil revenue?

a. 6.21%

b. 3.25%

c. 8.43%

d. 5.40%

e. 9.47%

QUESTION 18

Workforce UK's revenue and operating profit

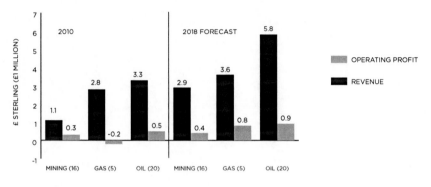

NUMBER AND TYPE OF COMPANIES OPERATING WITHIN "WORKFORCE UK"

What was the total operating profit per company from every sector combined in the year 2010?

a. £ 10,450

b. £ 9,985

c. £ 4,532

d. £ 13,834

e. £ 3,750

MOCK EXAM ANSWERS

1. b
2. b
3. e
4. d
5. c
6. e
7. e
8. d
9. a
10. a
11. d
12. e
13. d
14. d
15. b
16. a
17. e
18. e

MOCK EXAM
DETAILED ANSWERS

QUESTION 1 DETAILED ANSWER

2010 DRINK SALES IN SUPERMARKETS BY UK REGION (100,000s)

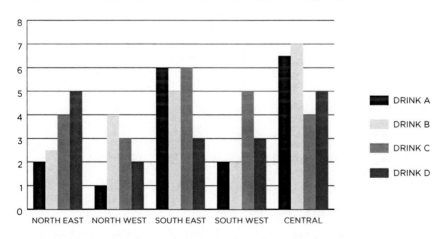

Total sales for all UK regions combined are a fifth of the sales of drink in supermarkets for the entire USA. If the south west region of the USA accounts for 30% of total USA drink sales in supermarkets, how many drinks were sold in south west USA in 2010?

The total drink sales for all UK regions combined are calculated by adding the sales from every region. So starting with the North East region, I read off the value of the sales from the graph and added them:

Calculate the total drink sales for each region in (100,000s):

North East = 2 + 2.5 + 4 + 5 = **13.5**

North West = 1 + 4 + 3 + 2 = **10**

South East = 6 + 5 + 6 + 3 = **20**

South West = 2 + 2 + 5 + 3 = **12**

Central = 6.5 + 7 + 4 + 5 = **22.5**

Total sales for all UK regions combined=**13.5+10+20+12+22.5**

=78 (100,000s)

Remember that all numbers have been divided by 100,000 to shorten them, which means that:

Total sales for all UK regions combined =78×100,000

=7,800,000

From the question, I know that the total sales for all UK regions combined are a fifth of the sales of drink in supermarkets for the entire USA:

$$\frac{1}{5} \times x = 7{,}800{,}000$$

$$x = 7{,}800{,}000 \times 5$$

Where x =Sales of drink in supermarkets for the entire USA

This means that:

Sales of drink in supermarkets for the entire USA=7,800,000×5

=39,000.000

The final part of the question states that:

"The south west region of the USA accounts for 30% of total USA drink sales in supermarkets".

To find how many drink sales in supermarkets took place in the South West region of the USA, simply multiply the total sales of drink in supermarkets for the entire USA by 30%.

Drinks sold in south west USA in 2010 $= \dfrac{30}{100} \times 39{,}000{,}000$

$$= 0.3 \times 39{,}000{,}000$$

$$= \mathbf{11{,}700{,}000}$$

Therefore **11,700,000** were sold in South West USA in 2010 and **b.** is the answer to question 1.

QUESTION 2 DETAILED ANSWER

2010 DRINK SALES IN SUPERMARKETS BY UK REGION (100,000s)

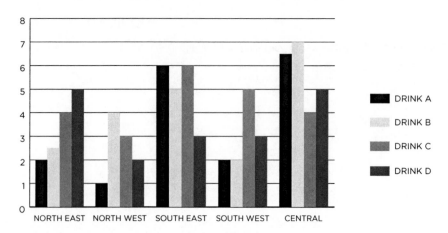

What percentage of total drinks sales from all regions combined did the South East and Central region approximately contain?

The first step towards solving this question is to find out what the total number of drink sales were.

(Note, that at this point if you had made notes and had the total sales for all UK regions combined written down from question 1 it would mean that you could skip the following step)

Calculate the total drink sales for each region in (100,000s):

North East = 2 + 2.5 + 4 + 5 = **13.5**

North West = 1 + 4 + 3 + 2 = **10**

South East = 6 + 5 + 6 + 3 = **20**

South West = 2 + 2 + 5 + 3 = **12**

Central = 6.5 + 7 + 4 + 5 = **22.5**

Total sales for all UK regions combined (in 100,000s)=**13.5+10+20+12+22.5**

=78

Remember that all numbers have been divided by 100,000 and multiplying

78 by 100,000 will give the actual total sales for all UK regions:

Total sales for all UK regions combined=78×100,000

=7,800,000

Next, I will need to know what the drink sales for the South East and Central region combined are. Once again, if notes are kept, this part of the question could be solved quicker than going back to the graph and working this out.

Total sales for South East and Central regions combined (in 100,000s)**=20+22.5**

=42.5

Again, remember that all numbers have been divided by 100,000 so that:

Total sales for South East and Central regions combined=**42.5×100,000**

=4,250,000

The final step is to find the percentage the South East and Central region occupies of the total drink sales for all UK regions combined:

TIP: *To calculate a percentage according to a total as required in this question, always make sure that the largest number is in the denominator (lower half) of the fraction and the smallest number is in the numerator (upper half) of the fraction.*

When using a calculator to solve the division this means typing the highest number in first then pressing the divide button followed by typing in the lowest number and finally pressing the equals button to get the result as a decimal. Multiplying this by 100 will give the result as a percentage.

$$\text{\% South East \& Central region occupies of the total sales} = \frac{4{,}250{,}000}{7{,}800{,}000} \times 100\%$$

$$=0.54487 \times 100\%$$

$$=54.49\%$$

The answer 54.49% can be rounded up to 54.5%

The answer to question 2 is **b. 54.5%**

Alternative method:

If you are not comfortable dealing with the larger numbers here is some good news. Because a percentage is required to be calculated in this question by dividing two numbers, both numbers could have been left shortened by 100,000.

So, rather than use **7,800,000** in all my calculations I could have used 78, which is 7,800,000 divided by 100,000. The key to using such a technique is to do exactly what is done with one number to the other. So, similarly, rather than use 4,250,000, I can divide this by 100,000 and then use 42.5 as shown below:

$$\% \text{ South East and Central region occupies of the total sale} = \frac{42.5}{78} \times 100\%$$

$$= 0.54487 \times 100\%$$

$$= 54.49\%$$

Once again, the answer 54.49% can be rounded up to 54.5%

The answer to question 2 is therefore **b. 54.5%**

QUESTION 3 DETAILED ANSWER

2010 DRINK SALES IN SUPERMARKETS BY UK REGION (100,000s)

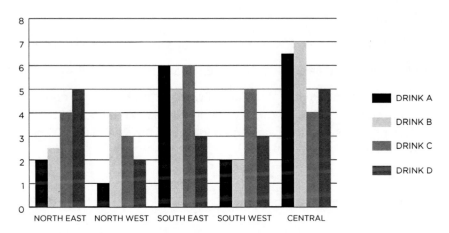

What was the total percentage increase for Drink's A and C combined when comparing North East and South East regional supermarket sales?

Here is the percentage increase formula again:

Percentage increase formula

   = [(*highest number - lowest number*) ÷ *lowest number*] × 100%

NOTE: It may be worth revisiting question 5 from the examples again if you had trouble with this question.

This means that to calculate a percentage increase, I will need both the highest and lowest numbers. For this question 'numbers' refer to the sales of drink's A and C in the North East and South East region.

Remember that the numbers in this graph have all been divided by 100,000 and therefore appear lower than they actually are. So for example, the number 2 on the graph actually represents the number 200,000

Be extra careful when reading numbers from the graph. Ensure that you do not use a combination such as North East sales for drink A is 2 and South East sales for drink A is 600,000. Be consistent and use both 2 for North East sales of drink A and 6 South East sales for drink A or use 200,000

North east sales of drink A and 600,000 South East sales for drink A. Both will get you the same result as shown below as long as you are consistent.

Starting with Drink A:

From the graph,

> Drink A North East sales=200,000 (or 2 if read straight from the graph)

> Drink A South East sales=600,000 (or 6 if read straight from the graph)

It is clear from the sales numbers that between North East sales and South East sales for drink A, the sales figure for the North East (200,000) is the lower number and the sales figure for the South East (600,000) is the higher number.

Remember,

> **% increase**=[(highest number - lowest number)÷lowest number] × 100%

So,

For drink A, the percentage increase of sales between the North East and South East regions can be calculated as:

% increase=[(highest number - lowest number)÷lowest number] × 100%

> =[(600,000–200,000)÷200,000]×100%

> =2×100%

> **=200%**

TIP: *Rather than have to type in all the zeros into your calculator, you could remove all 5 zeros from each number and carry out the calculation to get the same answer. It is important to ensure that the same amounts of zeros are removed from every number before carrying out the calculation. The best way of ensuring this is to read the numbers you require straight off from the graph (where the zeros have already been removed) and use those numbers to carry out the calculation as shown below.*

% increase=[(highest number - lowest number)÷lowest number] × 100%

> =[(6–2)÷2]×100%

> =2×100%

> **=200%**

Next, the same needs to be done for drink B and the percentage increase for drink B between the North East and South East regions can then be added to drink A's percentage increase to give the final answer.

Drink B:

From the graph,

> Drink B North East sales=400,000 (or 4 if read straight from the graph)

> Drink B South East sales=600,000 (or 6 if read straight from the graph)

TIME SAVING TIP: *If a 100% increase took place between North East and South East sales, in terms of the numbers this would mean a doubling of sales figures. So, if I were to increase the sales of Drink B North East by 100%, this would give drink B in the South East 800,000 sales, which is 400,000 more i.e. double sales compared to the North East for drink B.*

However, with the data obtained from the graph, Drink B South East sales has 600,000 sales which is a "600,000–400,000= 200,000" increase from Drink B North East sales.

If a 100% increase represents 400,000 more sales, then half this i.e. 200,000 more sales would represent a 50% increase in sales from Drink B North East to South East sales. This has saved doing a percentage increase calculation and the final answer can now be found by simply adding 50% to 200% to give 250%.

If you didn't manage to spot this don't panic. You need to be extra sharp to see it, especially when working under pressure. If your still not convinced that there is an increase of 50% between the two regions, it is best to go through the calculation using the formula, shown below.

For drink B, the percentage increase of sales between the North East and South East regions can be calculated as:

% increase= [(highest number - lowest number)÷lowest number] × 100%

$$=[(600,000-400,000)\div400,000]\times100\%$$

$$=0.5\times100\%$$

$$=50\%$$

Alternatively, carrying out the calculation using the numbers 4 and 6 read straight from the graph for drink C sales in the North East and South East regions respectively gives the same answer:

% increase=[(highest number-lowest number)÷lowest number]×100%

=[(6−4)÷4]×100%

=0.5×100%

=50%

The final step is to add both % increases, as the question asks for *"the total percentage increase for Drink's A and C combined"*:

Combined % increase for drinks A and C=200% + 50%

=**250%**

The final answer to question 3 is **e. 250%**

QUESTION 4 DETAILED ANSWER

Number of machines that need upgrading and location

LOCATION	NUMBER OF MACHINES THAT NEED UPGRADING	COST PER MACHINE REPLACED (£)
MIKES FACTORY	6,500	120
STEINER MANUFACTURING	3,300	95
CAPITAL MOTORS	860	310
MACHINERY FACTORY INC.	40	205

The first 500 machines that need upgrading will be replaced by 5 machines for every machine that needs to be upgraded.

The next 500 machines that need upgrading will be replaced by 3 machines for every machine that needs upgrading.

Any machines that need upgrading thereafter will be replaced by 2 machines for every machine that needs to be upgraded.

How many machines were replaced at Mikes Factory?

Answer

It is first necessary to understand how to find the number of replacement machines from the number of upgrades required and it is for this reason that the first part of the solution gives a thorough explanation on how to achieve this followed by how to apply the method to find the answer to question 4.

The box below the table gives a general formula for all machines that need upgrading. So, let's assume, for explanation purposes that there were **X** number of machines that need upgrading.

According to the passage inside the box, 'the first 500 machines that need upgrading will be replaced by 5 machines for every machine that needs to be upgraded'. A formula can be produced from this which is:

$$\text{Number of machines replaced} = 5 \times \textbf{\textit{X}}$$

Where **X** is the number of machines that need upgrading.

So, if for example, a company had 2 machines that need to be upgraded (**X**=2), the total number of machines that would be replaced in the company would be:

$$\text{Number of machines replaced (for 0 to 500 upgrades needed)} = 5 \times 2$$

$$= 10$$

This formula will only be valid up to a maximum of 500 machines that need upgrading i.e. the maximum value **X** can be here is 500.

If there are more than 500 machines that need upgrading, the passage inside the box beneath the table states: '**The next 500** machines that need upgrading will be replaced by **3** machines for every machine that needs upgrading'. Another formula can be produced here:

$$\text{Number of machines replaced (for 500 to 1000 upgrades needed)} = 3 \times \textbf{\textit{X}}$$

Remember, the first formula dealt with the FIRST 500 machines that needed upgrading and this formula deals with the NEXT 500 machines. In other words, it deals with machines that need upgrading from 500 to 1000 in quantity.

Below is an example of how to use both formulas:
Let's say a company had 800 machines that need to be upgraded, this lies between 500 and 1000. So, you will need to first calculate the machines replaced for the first 500 machines as shown below (**X**=500):

$$\text{Number of machines replaced (for 0 to 500 upgrades needed)} = 5 \times 500$$

$$= 2500$$

So the first 500 machines that require an upgrade will be replaced by 2,500 machines. This accounts for 500 machines out of the 800 that need upgrading. The numbers of machines that will replace the remaining 300 machines that need to be upgraded are calculated using the formula below where **X**=800−500=300:

$$\text{Number of machines replaced (for 500 to 1000 upgrades needed)} = 3 \times \textbf{\textit{X}}$$

$$= 3 \times 300$$

$$= 900$$

In total, the number of machines replacing those 800 machines that required an upgrade is:

$$\text{Total machines replaced} = 2500 + 900$$

$$= 3,400$$

So, 800 machines that required an upgrade will be replaced by a total of 3,400 machines

Referring to Mike's factory where 6,500 machines need to be upgraded. The first 500 machines that need to be upgraded require the following amount of replacement machines:

Number of machines replaced (for 0 to 500 upgrades needed) $= 5 \times 500$

$$= 2500$$

The NEXT 500 machines that need to be upgraded require the following amount of replacement machines ($X = 500$):

Number of machines replaced (for 500 to 1000 upgrades needed) $= 3 \times X$

$$= 3 \times 500$$

$$= 1500$$

The final part of the passage in the box states that: '**Any machines that need upgrading thereafter** will be replaced by **2** machines for every machine that needs to be upgraded'. This leads to the following formula:

Number of machines replaced (for 1000 to be upgraded or more) $= 2 \times X$

Where X is the remaining number of machines that need upgrading. This formula has no maximum value for X.

As I have calculated the number of replacement machines for the first 1,000 machines that require upgrading at Mike's factory, the remaining machines requiring an upgrade are:

Number of machines remaining that require upgrades $= 6,500 - 1,000$

$$= 5,500 \text{ Machines}$$

This means that the value of X in the formula will be 5,500:

Number of machines replaced (for 1000 to be upgraded or more) $= 2 \times X$

$$= 2 \times 5,500$$

$$= 11,000$$

Number of machines replaced at Mike's factory=2500+1500+11,000

=15,000 Machines replaced

There were 15,000 machines replaced in total at Mike's factory and the answer to question 4 is **d. 15,000**

QUESTION 5 DETAILED ANSWER

Number of machines that need upgrading and location

LOCATION	NUMBER OF MACHINES THAT NEED UPGRADING	COST PER MACHINE REPLACED (£)
MIKES FACTORY	6,500	120
STEINER MANUFACTURING	3,300	95
CAPITAL MOTORS	860	310
MACHINERY FACTORY INC.	40	205

The first 500 machines that need upgrading will be replaced by 5 machines for every machine that needs to be upgraded.

The next 500 machines that need upgrading will be replaced by 3 machines for every machine that needs upgrading.

Any machines that need upgrading thereafter will be replaced by 2 machines for every machine that needs to be upgraded.

How much would it cost to replace all the machines that need upgrading at Steiner manufacturing?

Answer

It is first necessary to calculate exactly how many machines will be replaced as a result of the requirement to upgrade 3,300 machines at Steiner manufacturing.

To find the number of machines that need to be replaced I will need to calculate the number of replacement machines for the first 500 machines that need to be upgraded at Steiner Manufacturing to start with using the following formula:

Number of machines replaced (for 0 to 500 upgrades needed)=5×500

=**2,500**

This formula is derived from the passage in the box beneath the table which states: '**The first 500** machines that need upgrading will be replaced by **5** machines for every machine that needs to be upgraded.'

The next step is to calculate the number of machines that will be replaced for the next 500 upgrades required and this is achieved using the following formula:

Number of machines replaced (for 500 to 1000 upgrades needed)=3×500

=1500

This formula is derived from the passage in the box beneath the table which states: '**The next 500** machines that need upgrading will be replaced by **3** machines for every machine that needs upgrading.'

In total, I have now calculated the number of replacement machines for the first 1000 upgrades required at Steiner Manufacturing. As there were 3,300 machines that required upgrading initially this means that there are still:

3,300−1,000=**2,300** machines which are required to be upgraded.

This is where I can use the final passage in the box beneath the table: '**Any machines that need upgrading thereafter** will be replaced by **2** machines for every machine that needs to be upgraded.'

Number of machines replaced (for 1000 to be upgraded or more)=2×2,300

=4,600

Number of machines replaced at Steiner manufacturing=2,500+1,500+4,600

=8,600

There were 8,600 machines replaced in total at Steiner manufacturing and at a cost of £95 per machine replaced, the total cost of replacing 8,600 works out to be:

Total cost of replacing 8,600 machines=8,600×£95

=£ 817,000

The answer to question 5 is **c. £ 817,000**

QUESTION 6 DETAILED ANSWER

Number of machines that need upgrading and location

LOCATION	NUMBER OF MACHINES THAT NEED UPGRADING	COST PER MACHINE REPLACED (£)
MIKES FACTORY	6,500	120
STEINER MANUFACTURING	3,300	95
CAPITAL MOTORS	860	310
MACHINERY FACTORY INC.	40	205

The first 500 machines that need upgrading will be replaced by 5 machines for every machine that needs to be upgraded.

The next 500 machines that need upgrading will be replaced by 3 machines for every machine that needs upgrading.

Any machines that need upgrading thereafter will be replaced by 2 machines for every machine that needs to be upgraded.

What is the total cost of replacing machines at all locations combined?

Answer

Important points to consider before answering this question

• The cost of replacing machines at Steiner manufacturing has already been calculated in question 5 and is £ 817,000

• The cost of replacing machines at Mike's factory can easily be calculated as the number of machines that will be replaced at Mike's factory was calculated in question 4 to be 15,000 machines replaced in total.

• All that needs to be done now to is multiply this by the cost per machine replaced (£) to find the total cost for replacing machines at Mike's factory.

TIP: *Question's like this, which make use of answers found in previous questions, often appear in numerical reasoning tests. It is for this reason that it* *is wise to keep notes on calculations and answers from the previous questions. This will save you time by not having to calculate the same thing again.*

Mike's factory total replacement machine costs

From the table, the cost of replacing a machine at Mike's factory is £120 which means that:

Total cost of replacing 15,000 machines at Mike's factory=15,000×£120

$$=£ 1,800,000$$

So far I have the cost of replacing the machines at Mike's factory and Steiner manufacturing.

This means that the cost of replacing machines at Capital Motors and Machinery factory inc. still need to be calculated.

Capital Motors total replacement machine costs

There are 860 machines that need upgrading. The first 500 machines that require an upgrade are replaced by the following number of machines:

Number of machines replaced (for 0 to 500 upgrades needed)=5×500

$$=2,500$$

There now remains:

860−500=360 machines that require an upgrade at Capital motors.

Because the number of machines to be replaced for the first 500 that required an upgrade has been calculated, the calculation for the remaining 360 machines will be done using the formula for anything from 500 to 1000 upgrades:

Number of machines replaced (for 500 to 1000 upgrades needed)=3×360

$$=1,080$$

Number of machines replaced at Capital Motors=2500+1,080

$$=3,580$$

From the table, the cost per machine replaced at Capital Motors is £ 310. So, if one replacement machine at Capital Motors costs £310, how much will 3,580 machines cost?

This can be found through a simple multiplication:

Total cost of replacing 3,580 machines at Capital Motors=3,580×£ 310

=£ 1,109,800

This means that 3,580 machines are replaced at Capital motors at a cost of £1,109,800.

This leads me onto the final location, Machinery Factory inc.

Machinery Factory Inc. Total replacement machine costs

There are 40 machines that need upgrading according to the table provided with the question. Therefore, the same formula used to calculate how many replacement machines are provided for the first 500 machines that require an upgrade will be used only as 40 is within the range 0 to 500:

Number of machines replaced (for 0 to 500 upgrades needed)= 5×40

=200

There are no further machines requiring an upgrade at Machinery Factory Inc. which means that the number of machines replaced at Machinery Factory Inc. is 200.

From the table, the cost per machine replaced at Machinery Factory Inc. is £205. So, if one replacement machine at Machinery Factory Inc. costs £205, how much will 200 machines cost?

This can be found through a simple multiplication as was done with Capital Motors:

Total cost of replacing 200 machines at Machinery Factory Inc=200×£205

=£ 41,000

This means that 200 machines are replaced at Machinery Factory Inc. at a cost of £41,000.

Finally, now that the individual costs for replacing machinery at every location have been calculated, it is possible to calculate the 'total cost of replacing machines at all locations combined' as the question requests by adding up each individual locations costs (highlighted in grey):

Total cost at all locations combined
=£ 817,000 (Steiner Manufacturing)

+£ 1,800,000 (Mike's Factory)

+£ 1,109,800 (Capital Motors)

+£ 41,000 (Machinery Factory Inc)

=£ 3,767,800

The final answer to question 6 is **e. £ 3,767,800**

TIP: *The multiple choice answers available to choose from contain two similar answers which are:*

a. £ 3,676,800 and e. £ 3,767,800

This technique is often used to test your ability to work under pressure. When under the pressure of being timed, it is very easy to confuse two numbers that appear so similar. Make sure you don't get caught out and double check that the answer you select is the answer that appears on your calculator display.

QUESTION 7 DETAILED ANSWER

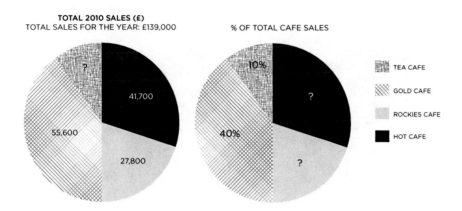

TOTAL 2010 SALES (£)
TOTAL SALES FOR THE YEAR: £139,000

% OF TOTAL CAFE SALES

TEA CAFE
GOLD CAFE
ROCKIES CAFE
HOT CAFE

What was the percentage of total sales for 'Rockies cafe' according to the 2010 sales figures?

Answer

There were £139,000 sales in total for the year 2010 by all the Cafe's combined. Rockies cafe contributed £27,800 towards this total, in other words, Rockies cafe contributed £27,800 out of the £139,000 total sales.

As a percentage, this would be:

$$\text{Percentage of total sales for 'Rockies cafe'} = \frac{£27,800}{£139,000} \times 100\%$$

$$= 0.2 \times 100\%$$

$$= \mathbf{20\%}$$

Therefore the percentage of total sales for 'Rockies cafe' according to the 2010 sales figures was **20%**. This is the answer to question 7.

QUESTION 8 DETAILED ANSWER

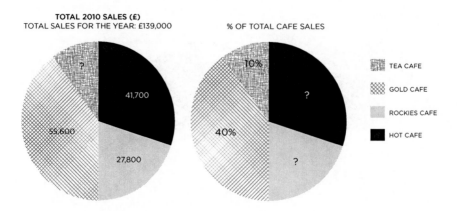

TOTAL 2010 SALES (£)
TOTAL SALES FOR THE YEAR: £139,000

% OF TOTAL CAFE SALES

TEA CAFE
GOLD CAFE
ROCKIES CAFE
HOT CAFE

What was the percentage of total sales for 'hot caf**e**'?

Answer

This question is very similar to question 7. 'Hot cafe' contributes £41,700 sales towards the total sales for the year 2010 which was £139,000.

As a percentage, this would be:

$$\text{Percentage of total sales for 'hot cafe'} = \frac{£41,700}{£139,000} \times 100\%$$

$$= 0.3 \times 100\%$$

$$= \mathbf{30\%}$$

Therefore the percentage of total sales for 'hot cafe' according to the 2010 sales figures was **30%.** This is the answer to question 8.

QUESTION 9 DETAILED ANSWER

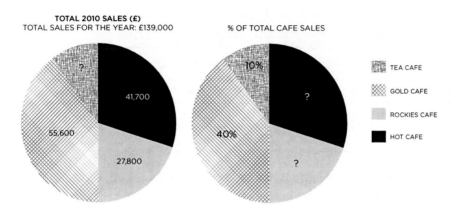

What was the 2010 sales figure for the 'tea cafe'?

Answer

Tea cafe, from the right hand pie chart, accounted for 10% of total cafe sales in 2010, which, from the pie chart on the left was £139,000 for the year 2010.

I need to establish how much the 'tea cafe' contributed towards the total sales figure and I can now do this knowing that it contributed 10% of the total sales figure:

TIP: *In mathematics, **of** means multiply.*

$$\text{2010 sales figure for the 'tea cafe'} = 10\% \times £\,139{,}000$$

$$= \frac{10}{100} \times £\,139{,}000$$

$$= 0.1 \times £\,139{,}000$$

$$= £\,13{,}900$$

The 2010 sales figure for the 'tea cafe' was **£ 13,900** and this is the answer to question 9.

QUESTION 10 DETAILED ANSWER

Today's exchange rates for dollars
(rates are stated as dollars per the currency listed)

	CLOSING POINT	TODAY'S HIGH	TODAY'S LOW	CLOSING POINT CHANGE FROM YESTERDAY
STERLING	35.21	36.31	33.18	+0.42
EURO	20.19	22.04	18.70	-0.32
YEN	0.25	0.28	0.23	+0.10

If the Today's high/ Closing point ratio for Yen is constant, what would 'Yesterday's high' for the Yen have been approximately?

Answer

The first step to take towards solving this question is to calculate the ratio

$$\frac{\textbf{(Today's high)}}{\textbf{Closing point}}$$

From the table, today's high for the yen is 0.28 and the closing point is 0.25, so the ratio using Yen becomes:

$$\frac{\textbf{(Today's high)}}{\textbf{Closing point}} = \frac{0.28}{0.25} = 1.12$$

The term 'Today's high' is valid today and the 'Today's high' of yesterday is actually 'yesterday's high'. The question is requesting 'Today's high' for the Yen Yesterday.

Considering that the table only provides information on the closing point change from yesterday, the only way that 'Yesterday's high' can be found is if the ratio remains constant, which it does. I can then put the term 'Today's high' in terms of closing point.

Today's high=1.12×closing point

Similarly, for yesterday this equation can be written as:

Yesterday s high=1.12×Yesterday s closing point

In order to calculate 'yesterday's high' I need to calculate what the closing point was in Yen yesterday. This is achieved as shown below:

Closing point change from yesterday (for Yen)=+0.10

This means that the closing point today has increased by 0.10 compared to yesterday's closing point value.

This means that if the closing point today is 0.25, simply subtract 0.1 from it to find yesterday's closing point.

Yesterday's closing point=0.25–0.10

=0.15

It is now possible to use yesterday's closing point value in Yen to calculate 'Yesterday's high' as I will be using yesterday's data to do the calculation.

Yesterday's high=1.12×Yesterday's closing point

=1.12×0.15

=0.168

This can now be rounded up to **0.17** which is the approximate value of Yesterday's high in Yen.

The answer to question 10 is a. **0.17**

QUESTION 11 DETAILED ANSWERS

Today's exchange rates for dollars
(rates are stated as dollars per the currency listed)

	CLOSING POINT	TODAY'S HIGH	TODAY'S LOW	CLOSING POINT CHANGE FROM YESTERDAY
STERLING	35.21	36.31	33.18	+0.42
EURO	20.19	22.04	18.70	-0.32
YEN	0.25	0.28	0.23	+0.10

A debt of £1,000,000 is owed and $45,000,000 was exchanged into Sterling at Today's high. Approximately how many pounds sterling would be leftover or still owing, if any, after paying the debt?

Answer

At todays high, there is $36.31 for every pound sterling as at the top of the table it mentions that *'rates are stated as dollars per currency listed'*.

If $36.31=£1 then how many pounds will $45,000,000 equal?

The quick way of doing this if you can see it is dividing $45,000,000 by $36.31, which will give you the value of $45,000,000 in pound sterling. However, if you can't see it not to worry, below is the method for solving this.

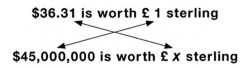

$36.31 is worth £ 1 sterling

$45,000,000 is worth £ x sterling

I now need to find £ sterling. This can be achieved by using cross multiplication and creating an equation as shown below:

$36.31×£ x=$45,000,000×£ 1

£ x=$45,000,000÷$36.31

=£ 1,239,328

After exchanging $45,000,000, there will be £1,239,328 available. Because a debt of £1,000,000 is owed I need to subtract £1,000,000 from this:

Pound Sterling available after debt is paid off=£ 1,239,328–£ 1,000,000

=£ 239,328

This is a left over amount as it is not negative and means that the amount of sterling that was available directly after an exchange at Today's high from dollars was higher than the amount owed. If the pound Sterling available after the debt is paid off was –£ 239.328, this would have meant that £ 239,328 is still owed. However, it is a positive number which means that £ 239,328 is left over.

The answer to question 11 is d. **£ 239,328 left over**

QUESTION 12 DETAILED ANSWERS

Today's exchange rates for dollars
(rates are stated as dollars per the currency listed)

	CLOSING POINT	TODAY'S HIGH	TODAY'S LOW	CLOSING POINT CHANGE FROM YESTERDAY
STERLING	35.21	36.31	33.18	+0.42
EURO	20.19	22.04	18.70	-0.32
YEN	0.25	0.28	0.23	+0.10

How many Euros would you get for £ 300 sterling yesterday, according to the closing point exchange rate (rounded to the nearest 10)?

Answer

This question requires a relationship between Euros and Sterling in order to find how many Euros one would get for £300 sterling. However, no such direct relationship exists, yet. In the solution below, I talk you through how to develop such a relationship in order to calculate the answer to this question.

For Euro's the closing point today is 20.19. This is down 0.32 from yesterday's value, which means I need to add 0.32 to today's Euro closing point value to find yesterday's closing point. Yesterday's closing point is calculated as shown below:

Yesterday's closing point (Euro)=20.19+0.32

=20.51

This means that yesterday's closing point exchange rate would give $19.87 per EURO.

At the same time, the closing point for Sterling today is 35.21, which is an increase of 0.42 from yesterday's closing point for sterling which means that I need to subtract 0.42 from today's closing point to find yesterday's closing point. Yesterday's closing point for sterling can be calculated as shown below:

Yesterday's closing point (Sterling)=35.21−0.42

=34.79

This means that yesterday's closing point exchange rate would give $34.79 per pound sterling.

This now leaves me with the following:

$20.51=1 EURO and

$34.79=£1 Sterling

Can you see what I have done here? I have built a relationship between pound sterling and Euros which cannot be found directly from the table by using dollars. In this case, the dollars act as a sort of messenger between Euro and Sterling as you will below. This will now enable me to complete the question.

The question asks *'How many Euros would you get for £ 300 sterling yesterday'*

Well, the only possible way to calculate this is to find how much £300 sterling is worth in dollars and then calculate how many Euros those dollars are worth. Everything has already been converted into yesterday's values so the calculation will automatically produce yesterday's exchange values.

$34.79 is worth £ 1 sterling

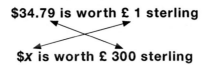

$x is worth £ 300 sterling

I now need to find the value of **$ x.** This can be achieved by using cross multiplication and creating an equation as shown below:

$$\$x \times £\ 1 = \$34.79 \times £\ 300$$

$$\$x = \$10,437$$

So using yesterday's closing point exchange rate, £300 sterling was worth $10,437

I will now need to find how many Euro's $10,437 was worth. This is achieved using the relationship I calculated earlier in the solution, which was:

$20.51=1 EURO

$20.51 is worth 1 EURO

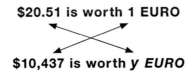

$10,437 is worth y EURO

I now need to find the value of **y EURO**. This can be achieved by using cross multiplication and creating an equation as shown below:

$$\$10,437 \times 1 \text{ EURO} = \$20.51 \times y \text{ EURO}$$

$$y \text{ EURO} = \frac{\$10,437 \times 1 \text{ EURO}}{\$20.51}$$

$$= \frac{\$10,437}{\$20.51} \text{ EURO}$$

$$= 508.87 \text{ EURO}$$

This is equivalent to 508.9, which when rounded up to a whole number becomes 509. Rounding 509 to the nearest 10 as requested in the question would give **e. 510 EURO's** as the answer.

The answer to question 12 is that £300 sterling when exchanged at yesterday's closing point is worth 510 EURO's (rounded to the nearest 10).

QUESTION 13

TIME TAKEN TO TRAVEL HOME FROM WORK

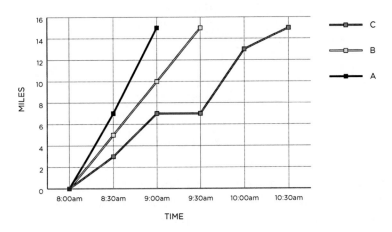

100 miles = 161 km

If Danny's train leaves at 8.30am rather than 8am and maintained an average speed of 48.3 km/h throughout the journey to work without any delays, what time would Danny arrive at work?

Answer

An average speed of 48.3km/h needs to be converted from km per hour into miles per hour.

This is achieved using the conversion given in the question,

100 miles=161 km

Danny's train is covering 48.3km every hour. To convert this into miles I use the following cross multiplication technique

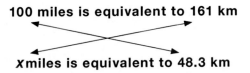

100 miles is equivalent to 161 km

Xmiles is equivalent to 48.3 km

I now need to find the value of **Xmiles**. This can be achieved by using cross multiplication and creating an equation as shown below:

$$X\text{ miles} \times 161 \text{ km} = 100 \text{ miles} \times 48.3 \text{ km}$$

$$X\text{ miles} = \frac{100 \times 48.3}{161}$$

$$= \frac{4830}{161}$$

$$= 30 \text{ miles}$$

This means that Danny's train covers a distance of 30 miles every hour and is therefore travelling at an average speed of 30 miles per hour.

The distance from Danny's home train station to his workplace is 15 miles and if the train is covering 30 miles in an hour, how much distance would it cover in half this time if there were no delays? It would be half the distance it would cover in one hour, in other words 15 miles.

Therefore, if Danny's train left at 8.30am travelling at a speed of 48.3km/h (30 mph) it would reach his work place which is 15 miles away in half an hour, which means that Danny would arrive at work for 9.00am, exactly half an hour after he began the train journey.

The answer to question 13 is **d. 9.00am**

QUESTION 14 DETAILED ANSWER

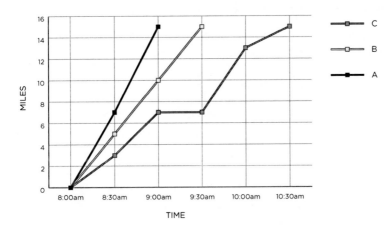

TIME TAKEN TO TRAVEL HOME FROM WORK

100 miles = 161 km

At 112.63 km from Sam's house, the bus encountered mechanical failure and Sam had to wait from 9am to 9.30am for a replacement bus to arrive so that he could complete his journey to work. If the bus had not broken down and kept the same average speed as it did from 8am to 9am, approximately what time would Sam have arrived at work?

Answer

From the graph it should be clear where the break down had occurred. It will be the part where no miles are covered and where time has moved on, as seen between 9am to 9.30am for Sam's bus. However, the question has kindly informed me of both the location and time of the incident so there should be no confusion with this.

To calculate what time Sam would have arrived at work had his bus maintained the same average speed between 8am to 9am and not broken down, it is necessary to first calculate what the average speed of the bus was between 8am and 9am. This is achieved by using the equation:

$$\text{Speed} = \frac{\text{distance}}{\text{time}}$$

The distance the bus covered between 8am and 9am can be found by simply reading off the graph at 9am because at 8am, the bus had covered 0 miles and by 9am it had covered 7 miles.

The time this took was 1 hour (8am to 9am).

Using these numbers, it is possible to calculate the average speed of the bus from 8am to 9am as shown below:

$$\text{Speed} = \frac{\text{distance}}{\text{time}}$$

$$= \frac{7 \text{ miles}}{1 \text{ hour}}$$

$$= 7 \text{ miles per hour (mph)}$$

If the bus travelled at this speed for the entire journey, without any disruptions, how long would it take to cover 15 miles? The answer to this can be found using the following method:

Remember, **60 minutes =1 hour**

The bus covers 7 miles in 60 minutes

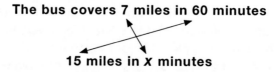

15 miles in X minutes

I now need to find the value of **X minutes**. This can be achieved by using cross multiplication and creating an equation as shown below:

X minutes×7 miles=60 minutes×15 miles

$$\text{X minutes} = \frac{60 \times 15}{7}$$

$$= \frac{900}{7}$$

$$= 128.57$$

This is rounded up to approximately 129 minutes. To convert this into hours, if 60 minutes is 1 hour then 120 minutes is 2 hours which means that 129 minutes is 2 hours 9 minutes.

If Sam started his journey to work by bus at 8am, he would have arrived at his workplace 2 hours 9 minutes later, 10.09 am

The answer to question 14 is **d. 10.09am**

QUESTION 15 DETAILED ANSWER

TIME TAKEN TO TRAVEL HOME FROM WORK

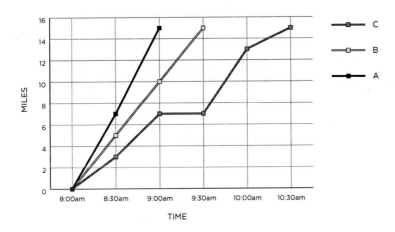

100 miles = 161 km

At 8.30am, Anita receives a call from her boss telling her to be at work for 9am. What is the minimum speed Anita would need to drive at, in km/h from 8.30am onwards in order to be at work for 9am?

Answer

At 8.30am Anita has already covered 5 miles of her 15 mile journey to work by car. This means that 10 miles still need to be covered and in order to be at work for 9am Anita needs to cover those remaining 10 miles within half an hour. The reason why a minimum speed is asked for is because a speed will be calculated for Anita which will get her to work at exactly 9am. Any speed above the minimum speed would get her to work earlier than 9am and any speed below the minimum speed would make her late.

Once again, the equation **Speed=$\dfrac{\text{distance}}{\text{time}}$** will need to be used as shown below:

Remember

- Distance Anita needs to cover is 10 miles

- She has half an hour to do this in which is 0.5 hour in decimal form (necessary for calculations)

$$Speed = \frac{distance}{time}$$

$$= \frac{10 \text{ miles}}{0.5 \text{ hour}}$$

$$= 20 \text{ miles per hour (mph)}$$

If Anita drives at 20 mph from 8.30am onwards she will arrive at work at exactly 9am. The question requests this speed to be in km/h. To convert 20 mph into km/h use the following method:

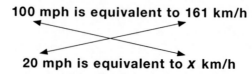

100 mph is equivalent to 161 km/h

20 mph is equivalent to *x* km/h

I now need to find the value of *x* km/h. This can be achieved by using cross multiplication and creating an equation as shown below:

x km/h×100 mph=161 km/h×20 mph

$$x \text{ km/h} = \frac{161 \times 20}{100}$$

$$= \frac{3220}{100} \text{ km/h}$$

$$= 32.2 \text{ km/h}$$

The answer to question 15 is **b. 32.2 km/h**

QUESTION 16 DETAILED ANSWER

Workforce UK's revenue and operating profit

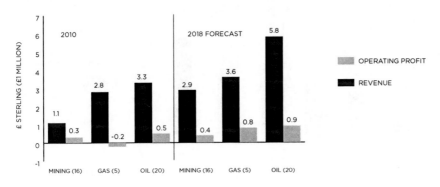

NUMBER AND TYPE OF COMPANIES OPERATING WITHIN "WORKFORCE UK"

What is the forecasted percentage increase in Revenue for the Gas industry between 2010 and 2018?

Answer

This question requires the use of the percentage increase formula and just in case you need to see it again, here it is:

Percentage increase formula

=[(highest number - lowest number) ÷ lowest number] × 100%

For this particular question, the percentage increase can be written as:

=[(highest revenue - lowest revenue) ÷ lowest revenue] × 100%

In 2010 gas revenue was **2.8 million** and the 2018 forecasted revenue is **3.6 million.**

The percentage increase between the 2010 revenue and the 2018 forecasted revenue is:

%increase=[(highest revenue-lowest revenue)÷lowest revenue] × 100%

   =[(3.6 million−2.8 million)÷2.8 million]×100%

   =(0.8 million÷2.8 million)×100%

   =0.286×100%

   =28.6%

The answer to question 16 is **a. 28.6%**

QUESTION 17 DETAILED ANSWER

Workforce UK's revenue and operating profit

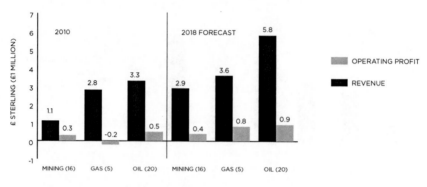

NUMBER AND TYPE OF COMPANIES OPERATING WITHIN "WORKFORCE UK"

What will be the annual percentage increase in the Oil industries revenue, taking into account the total increase between the 2010 oil revenue and 2018 forecasted oil revenue?

Answer

This question is asking what the annual percentage increase in oil revenue works out to be per year. Once again, the percentage increase formula will need to be used to answer this question.

In 2010 oil revenue was **3.3 million** and the 2018 forecasted revenue is **5.8 million.**

The percentage increase between the 2010 revenue and the 2018 forecasted revenue is:

%increase=[(highest revenue-lowest revenue)÷lowest revenue] × 100%

=[(5.8 million−3.3 million)÷3.3 million]×100%

=(2.5 million÷3.3 million)×100%

=0.7576×100%

=7576.%

The period between 2010 and 2018 spans 8 years, so the % increase per year in oil revenue would be the total % increase in oil revenue between

2010 and 2018 forecasted revenue increase divided by 8.

%increase in oil revenue per year=75.76%÷8

=9.47%

The answer to question 17 is **e. 9.47%**

QUESTION 18

Workforce UK's revenue and operating profit

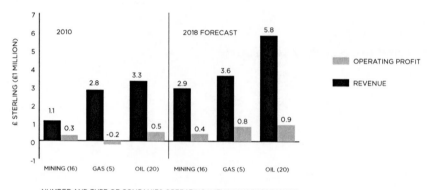

NUMBER AND TYPE OF COMPANIES OPERATING WITHIN "WORKFORCE UK"

What was the total operating profit per company from every sector combined in the year 2010?

Answer

The number of companies are displayed in brackets next to type of company on the x-axis e.g. Mining has 16 in brackets next to it as there are 16 companies that conduct mining activities.

In 2010, the total operating profit from all companies combined for mining was 0.3 million. There are 16 companies in mining and so to find the operating profit per company simply divide 0.3 million (300,000) by 16.

$$\text{Operating profit per mining company in 2010}(\pounds) = \frac{300,000}{16}$$

$$= \pounds\,18,750$$

Next up are Gas companies. There are 5 gas companies that generated a total negative operating profit of 0.2 million in 2010. Once again, to find the operating profit per company simply divide –0.2 million (–200,000) by 5.

$$\text{Operating profit per gas company in 2010}(\pounds) = \frac{-200,000}{5}$$

$$= -\pounds\,40,000$$

Finally Oil has 20 companies and in total these 20 companies generated an operating profit of 0.5 million in 2010. Once again, to find the operating profit per company simply divide 0.5 million (500,000) by 20.

$$\text{Operating profit per oil company in 2010(£)} = \frac{500,000}{20}$$

$$= £\ 25,000$$

The total operating profit per company combined in the year 2010 can be found by adding up the individual company operating profits from all three sectors (numbers highlighted in grey).

Total operating profit per company combined=£ 18,750– £ 40,000+ £ 25,000

$$= +£\ 3,750$$

The answer to question 18 is **e. £ 3,750**

This concludes the detailed answers to the mock exam.

If you have been through the entire book, congratulate yourself because as a result you are now in a much better position to tackle advanced numerical reasoning tests. Well done.

If you liked this book please tell your friends, family, colleagues, acquaintances or anyone for that matter.

I can also personally recommend visiting **www.how2become.co.uk** for more inspirational guides and practice psychometric questions which will no doubt help you further towards gaining your perfect job.

I wish you every success with your job hunt from here onwards and I hope I have helped you on your journey to success.

David Isaacs
Author

For other products
and online tests by

DAVID ISAACS

please visit:

GCSEPracticePapers.com

how2become

Visit www.how2become.co.uk to find more titles and courses that will help you to pass any career selection process:

- 1 Day intensive training courses
- Job interview DVD's and books
- Online numerical tests
- Psychometric testing books and CDs

WWW.HOW2BECOME.CO.UK

 THE **TESTING** SERIES